Make
Things
Happen!

D0531487

The Quest Toolbox Series

This series is different. It provides practical techniques, tested by experienced consultants with real organisations. Each tool follows a step-by-step approach, illustrated by worked examples. No theoretical explanations, just a wide choice of techniques to help stimulate, drive and manage change and the people that create it. Hundreds of directors, managers and team leaders worldwide are already using the series for personal reference, as handout material for training programmes or as an aid for project or improvement teams.

Steve Smith

Dr Smith has been helping organisations transform their performance and culture for 20 years. His unique experience of witnessing and consulting in global corporate change has helped him become regarded as one of the most progressive change management consultants of his generation.

A regular speaker and author, as well as conceptual thinker, Steve has facilitated the metamorphosis of over 150 organisations through the provision of timely, supportive and often pioneering consultancy advice.

A strong advocate of an holistic approach to business improvement, Steve works with his clients to define stretching, yet balanced strategies that work, and then helps to mobilise the whole organisation to turn those strategies into action.

Prior to forming Quest, Steve was a director of PA Consulting Services, where he worked for 11 years and founded the TQM division. A former lecturer at Aston University, Steve has also spent eight years with the Chrysler Corporation.

Acknowledgements

The Toolbox series has been drawn from the expertise of the entire Quest Worldwide consultancy team. Special thanks must go to Gillian Hayward for selecting and compiling tools for all five titles and to Mike Rayburn who developed and refined many of the techniques in *Make Things Happen!* Thanks also to Peter Holman, Tina Jacobs, Sue Hodder and the Quest support team.

Make Things Happen!

Readymade Tools for Project Improvement

Edited by
Steve Smith

**KOGAN
PAGE**

QUEST QUALITY

YOURS TO HAVE AND TO HOLD
BUT NOT TO COPY

The publication you are reading is protected by copyright law. This means that the publisher could take you and your employer to court and claim heavy legal damages if you make unauthorised photocopies from these pages. Photocopying copyright material without permission is no different from stealing a magazine from a newsagent, only it doesn't seem like theft.

The Copyright Licensing Agency (CLA) is an organisation which issues licences to bring photocopying within the law. It has designed licensing services to cover all kinds of special needs in business, education and government.

If you take photocopies from books, magazines and periodicals at work your employer should be licensed with the CLA. Make sure you are protected by a photocopying licence.

The Copyright Licensing Agency Limited, 90 Tottenham Court Road, London W1P 0LP. Tel: 0171 436 5931. Fax: 0171 436 3986.

First published in 1997

Apart from any fair dealing for the purposes of research or private study, or criticism or review, as permitted under the Copyright, Designs and Patents Act 1988, this publication may only be reproduced, stored or transmitted, in any form or by any means, with the prior permission in writing of the publishers, or in the case of reprographic reproduction in accordance with the terms and licences issued by the CLA. Enquiries concerning reproduction outside those terms should be sent to the publishers at the undermentioned address:

Kogan Page Limited
120 Pentonville Road
London N1 9JN

© Quest Worldwide Education Ltd

The right of Quest Worldwide Education Ltd to be identified as author of this work has been asserted by them in accordance with the Copyright, Designs and Patents Act 1988.

British Library Cataloguing in Publication Data

A CIP record for this book is available from the British Library.

ISBN 0 7494 2484 2

Typeset by Florencetype Ltd, Stoodleigh, Devon
Printed in England by Clays Ltd, St Ives plc

Contents

"A project is a problem scheduled for solution"

J M Juran (Quality Guru)

"A project is a one-time job that has defined starting and ending dates, a clearly specified objective, or scope of work to be performed, a pre-defined budget, and usually a temporary organisation that is dismantled once the project is complete."

James P Lewis (Project Guru)

A project in context

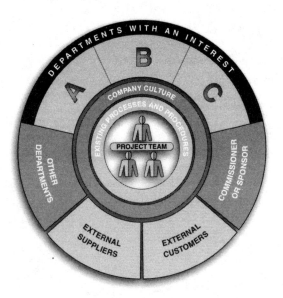

A project is not simply a process, or a one-off event. A project has to be seen as a set of activities taking place for a finite period within an existing system. However, a project can also impact upon, or even change quite drastically, the existing system or order of things. As a consequence, whoever leads or manages a project team has to take account of existing constraints and differing demands as well as the implications for any changes which might follow.

The better defined, planned, executed and controlled your projects are, the more likely it will be that they will achieve business improvement efficiently and effectively.

This Toolbox gives you a wide range of practical tools that you can use through the life cycle of a project to:

- increase your chance of success

- improve your efficiency

- reduce your stress level

- help you get things done faster and better.

The Toolbox is aimed primarily at improvement projects and therefore touches only very lightly on the financial and budgetary aspects of large-scale capital projects. The emphasis is deliberately on performance improvement through the focused use of the skills and abilities of the people who are responsible for performing the work and implementing the process.

While this Toolbox is paper-based, it does not mean that all of the tools have to be so. Be creative and use computers to give you more speed and flexibility. You'll be surprised how quickly you can

"Make things happen!"

 A PROJECT SHOULD HAVE A PRECISE BEGINNING, IDENTIFIABLE MIDDLE AND A DEFINITE END

How to use this Toolbox

What it is

This Toolbox is made up of practical tools to help you set up and run successful projects. It is structured around the five phases of project management:

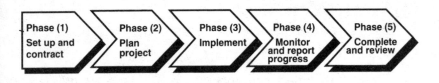

Phase (1)	Phase (2)	Phase (3)	Phase (4)	Phase (5)
Set up and contract	Plan project	Implement	Monitor and report progress	Complete and review

There are also additional sections in the Toolbox dealing with:

- An overview of project management.

- Selecting a project.

- Managing multi-projects.

Each tool includes a description of:

- What it is.

- How to use it.

- How it helps.

In order to illustrate the tools, examples have been developed from various fictional companies including O'Faro Ltd and Global Gnomes Inc.

How to use it

1. Before starting a project, consider the scale and scope of the issue(s) you will be tackling. Larger projects require greater resources, support, determination and discipline. Smaller ones require a lighter touch but still need careful managing.

| | Implications | | | |
Scale of project	Type of team	Impact	Resources needed	Management required
Small eg removing specific causes of waste in a production cell or administrative procedure	Small number of operators involved in the process, often having frequent, ad-hoc meetings in the workplace	Departmental Short timescale – should be completed in weeks	Limited to small amount of time and existing facilities	Local manager acts as combined commissioner and sponsor Oral rather than written reporting Storyboard displayed in area
Medium eg developing new performance management system or introducing e-mail	Larger number of functional representatives meeting formally at discrete intervals. Senior and middle management represented	Cross-functional Likely to take several months	Significant amounts of management time particularly duing implementation. May require external expertise and have systems implications Could require capital expenditure	Should have board level sponsor although leader will be less senior Regular written reports needed by sponsor Once completed, will need thorough communication to a wide audience
Major eg supply chain re-engineering or greenfield site development	Senior steering team with a range of sub-teams during the life of the project	Organisation-wide Over a year or more	Capital expenditure and external experts likely. Significant impact on budgets, systems and resources	Commissioned by Board who are all actively involved. Board level sponsor Regular reporting to Board and widespread communication across the organisation

2. The tools you select to manage the project will vary according to scale and scope. Use the table on the following page to help you select the most appropriate tools for the scale of your project.

3. You can also use this Toolbox to help you tackle specific steps in existing projects. Review the index to identify the best fit for your need.

4. Once you have chosen which tool(s) to use, simply follow the 'how to use it' instructions.

Tools \ Scale of project	Small	Medium	Major
Project brief	✔	✔	✔
Issue statement	✔	✔	✔
Mission and key objectives	✔	✔	✔
Required outputs and timing	✔	✔	✔
Scope and limits		✔	✔
Budget		✔	✔
Roles	✔	✔	✔
Personal contracts		✔	✔
Project contract		✔	✔
Project management plan		✔	✔
PLAN-DO-CHECK-ACT	✔	✔	✔
Breakdown structure			✔
Key activity and task plan	✔	✔	✔
Responsibility chart		✔	✔
Resource requirement list		✔	✔
Cost breakdown structure		✔	✔
Gantt chart	✔		
CPA		✔	✔
Contingency plan			✔
Support implementation	✔	✔	✔
Progress reports	✔ (verbal)	✔	✔
Project log			✔
Review meetings		✔	✔
Sort out problems	✔	✔	✔
Change procedure			✔
Analyse deviations	✔	✔	✔
Pre-completion review			✔
Cost benefit analysis	✔	✔	✔
Presentation	✔	✔	✔
Complete the work	✔	✔	✔
Handover		✔	✔
Celebrate!	✔	✔	✔
Post-completion review			✔

5. Review your success as you go and make a note of any specific points that could be useful next time you need a tool.

How it helps

Projects can be complex and demanding. This Toolbox gives you a broad range of simple, practical, easy to use tools to break your task into manageable chunks.

HINT! YOU CAN EAT AN ELEPHANT ONE BITE AT A TIME

Tools index

5 Implement

6 Monitor and report progress

7 Complete and review

8 Manage multi-projects

1 Overview

Projects and Processes

What it is

There are four ways in which a project can be viewed. A project:

- is a process in its own right as it has inputs, outputs and activities in between
- should use an analytical process such as PLAN–DO–CHECK–ACT
- usually analyses other processes such as manufacturing, administration, product development, etc
- requires a management process to plan and control what is happening.

Project as a process

A project can be viewed as a series of events or activities which are usually connected or related.

```
┌─────────┐     ┌─────────┐     ┌─────────┐
│  Event  │ ──▶ │  Event  │ ──▶ │  Event  │
│    1    │     │    2    │     │    3    │
└─────────┘     └─────────┘     └─────────┘
```

However, a project goes beyond just sequencing. It involves converting inputs into outputs to produce a pre-defined result.

Project as a user of an analytical process

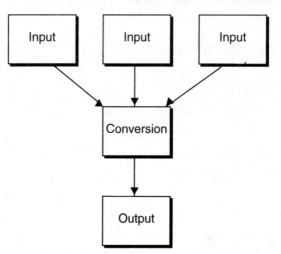

A project normally deals either with problems or performance improvements and should use an analytical process to do so. The *improvement process* is a disciplined combination of techniques for tackling a problem and/or securing an improvement. It is based on the PLAN-DO-CHECK-ACT Cycle.

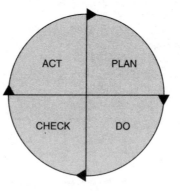

The four stages can be broken into 13 steps as shown on the next page.

A systematic improvement process:

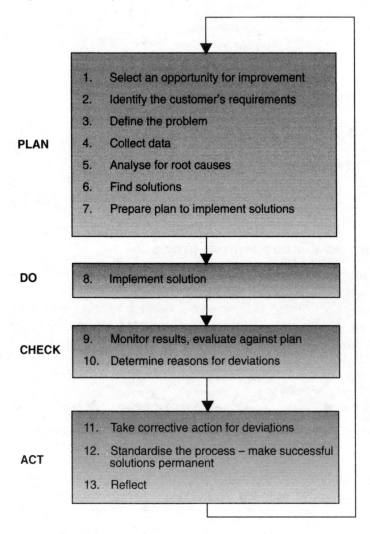

PLAN

1. Select an opportunity for improvement
2. Identify the customer's requirements
3. Define the problem
4. Collect data
5. Analyse for root causes
6. Find solutions
7. Prepare plan to implement solutions

DO

8. Implement solution

CHECK

9. Monitor results, evaluate against plan
10. Determine reasons for deviations

ACT

11. Take corrective action for deviations
12. Standardise the process – make successful solutions permanent
13. Reflect

Project as an 'analyser' of other processes

Projects usually involve looking at existing processes in the business; either a specific process in a particular area, or a process which cuts across several functional or departmental boundaries.

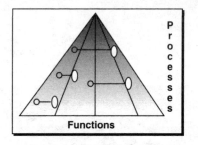

Many project teams are cross-functional or multi-disciplinary, simply because they are dealing with cross-functional processes.

Other processes may involve suppliers and customers which may mean the project team has to include outside representatives.

Project as a management process

A project needs managing and this demands additional disciplines to those for analysing the problem or process. This Toolbox incorporates planning and monitoring tools which are essential for effective project management through the five phases in the life of a project.

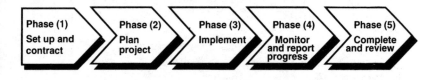

The foldout at the back of this Toolbox shows the links between the improvement process, the project management process and the sections in this Toolbox.

How to use it

1. Before embarking on your project ask yourself:

- Are you clear on what you need to do?
    - have you clarified your inputs and outputs?
    - have you defined the main steps in-between?

- Are you clear how you are going to tackle the work?

  - make sure you are familiar with PLAN-DO-CHECK-ACT

  - get a copy of Quest's *Solve that problem!* Toolbox and be ready to use specific tools along the way.

- Have you agreed which process(es) you are going to be improving/developing/investigating?

  - do they cross functional boundaries?

  - are you working at a macro or micro level?

  - are the main players aware/involved?

- Have you taken steps to ensure you can effectively manage the project?

  - how will you know where you are in your plan?

  - how will you know how much resource is used/left?

  - how will you keep others informed?

2. If you are happy with your responses to these questions your four project processes must be clear and under control. If you are not, use the relevant sections of this Toolbox to ensure you have covered them all.

How it helps

Tackling projects in terms of the four key processes will help to ensure you know what you're doing, you have a means of achieving it and you know how you're doing.

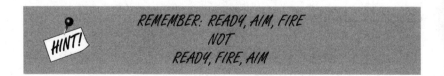

HINT!

REMEMBER: READY, AIM, FIRE
NOT
READY, FIRE, AIM

Potential Pitfalls and Prevention Checklist

What it is

This tool outlines the common mistakes that are made when managing projects. It goes on to give a prevention checklist showing what you can do to avoid the pitfalls and build in success.

How to use it

1. Review the following list of project pitfalls. Which of them are true of your project? What are the consequences?

Policy level

✗ Insufficient support for project

- project plans not aligned with business plans

✗ Poor project definition

- goals of project not clear
- limits of scope not defined

Planning

✗ Planning level is uniform, ie does not apply 'high level' and detail to management and operational activities respectively

✗ Planning tools are too complex and unwieldy

✗ Planning timescale is too long

✗ Planning method discourages creativity

✗ Planning of time and cost are over-optimistic

✗ Planning of resources overestimates competence and capacity

✗ Project schedule ignores lost time

Organisation

✗ The organisational 'fit' of the project is not considered

✗ Distribution of responsibility is not defined

✗ Principles of cooperation are unclear

✗ Key resources are not available when required

✗ Key resources are not motivated

✗ Line managers are not committed

✗ Communication is poor

✗ Project leader is a specialist rather than a manager and so finds it difficult to delegate, support, coordinate and control

Control

✗ Project leader and team do not understand the purpose of control, or the difference between monitoring and controlling

✗ Planning and progress reports are not integrated

✗ There is no well defined, formalised communication between project leader and project members

✗ The project leader has responsibility but no authority

Implementation

✗ Complexity of coordinating a multitude of resources is underestimated

✗ Changes to the plan or specification are uncontrolled

✗ Activities are not completed and documented before others begin

✗ Targets of time, cost and quality are unbalanced

2. Now review the prevention checklist:

✔ **Focus on results** ☐

- Align the project plan with the business plan
- Define the principles and policies of project work
- Maintain the support of the project's champion and sponsor
- Clarify the boundaries and scope of the project
- Set criteria for success

✔ **Layer the plans** ☐

- Develop a plan that is robust but flexible
- Define intermediate goals to control time, cost and quality
- Do all the work in the right order
- Use simple, comprehensive tools for planning and control

✔ **Plan creatively** ☐

- Involve project members
- Account for the competence, capacity and availability of resources
- Create an understanding that change takes time and absorbs resources

✔ **Organise the project** ☐

- Adopt a structure that is flexible and apt
- Define roles and responsibilities
- Communicate effectively

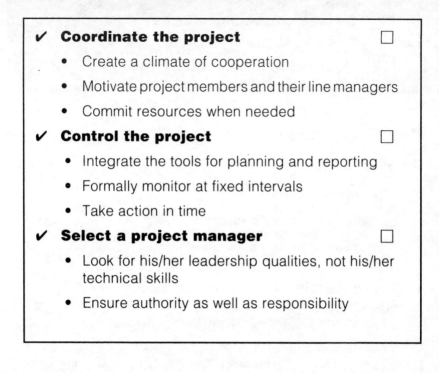

✔ **Coordinate the project** ☐

- Create a climate of cooperation
- Motivate project members and their line managers
- Commit resources when needed

✔ **Control the project** ☐

- Integrate the tools for planning and reporting
- Formally monitor at fixed intervals
- Take action in time

✔ **Select a project manager** ☐

- Look for his/her leadership qualities, not his/her technical skills
- Ensure authority as well as responsibility

3. Which of these things have you done?

4. Which of these things have you not done?

5. Use the remainder of the Toolbox to help you identify actions to improve your approach to projects.

How it helps

Prevention is better than cure. This tool will help you to plan for success rather than have to react to problems and pitfalls.

2 Select your project

Capture Ideas

What it is

Projects originate in three ways:

- Somebody has a good idea.

- A problem arises or keeps recurring which can no longer be ignored.

- An improvement in performance is needed, for example in response to competitor action, or customer demand, or as a requirement of the strategic plan.

Companies cannot afford to lose good ideas or OFIs (opportunities for improvement). The initial problem is deciding which ones to go for first, bearing in mind there are finite resources and perceived limits on capacity to absorb change.

This means that disciplines should be attached to project origination, both to ensure good ideas do not go begging and to provide a sound basis for vetting and selection. This tool outlines the key characteristics of a project origination process.

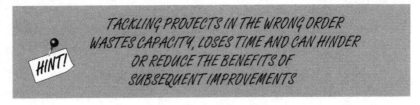

HINT!

TACKLING PROJECTS IN THE WRONG ORDER WASTES CAPACITY, LOSES TIME AND CAN HINDER OR REDUCE THE BENEFITS OF SUBSEQUENT IMPROVEMENTS

How to use it

1. Define the purpose of the project origination process. For example, to trawl and gather effectively all constructive suggestions, ideas and problems which could form the subject matter of future projects.

2. Develop a simple procedure to capture and evaluate the topics from which projects will be chosen.

   The following elements need to be considered:

   - The procedure itself
     - local/company-wide?
     - paper/electronic?
   - Roles
     - who will administer?
     - who will make decisions?
     - who will maintain procedure/database?
   - Briefing/training
     - how to ensure widespread awareness of its purpose and process?
     - how to ensure everyone (on an ongoing basis) is able to use the procedure?
   - Measures
     - what criteria will be used to assess OFIs?
     - how will the overall process be tracked, eg % participation?

> **HINT!** *A COMPANY IN WHICH IDEAS ARE ENCOURAGED AND FREELY GENERATED, PROBLEMS OPENLY IDENTIFIED AND IMPROVEMENTS CONTINUOUSLY SOUGHT, WILL UNLEASH A RICH FLOW OF IMPROVEMENT ENERGY*

3. Design a simple to use proposal form – an example is shown overleaf – and make sure it's widely available (either on paper or electronically).

4. Ensure all proposal forms are collected by people empowered and trained to select, decide, authorise, implement and monitor proposed OFIs. Make sure there is a company-wide, consistent procedure for handling them.

How it helps

By defining a process for capturing and evaluating potential improvement projects, you ensure that:

- everyone has the opportunity to contribute

- good ideas are not lost

- timely and logical decisions are made on which projects to progress

- resource is focused on the most useful improvement activities.

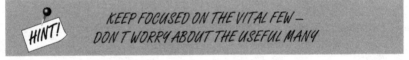

HINT!

KEEP FOCUSED ON THE VITAL FEW – DON'T WORRY ABOUT THE USEFUL MANY

An example of a form used to propose an improvement project is shown on the next page.

IMPROVEMENT TEAM PROPOSAL

Part 1 – to be completed by proposer

From (proposer):_____   Department: _____

To (line manager): _____   Date: _____

Idea, problem, Opportunity for Improvement: _____

Anticipated benefits of tackling this OFI: _____

Measure(s) of success: _____

Part 2 – to be completed by line manager

	Yes ✔	No ✗
This proposal is within my authority:	☐	☐
This proposal is approved:	☐	☐

Agreed sponsor:_____

Agreed team leader: _____

Agreed facilitator: _____

This proposal is declined because:

_____

_____

_____

This proposal is not within my authority and is hereby forwarded to:

_____

_____

Signed: _____

Select Which One(s) To Do

What it is

This tool gives alternative methods for selecting which projects to do out of the range of those proposed.

Those who authorise a project ('project commissioners' – see later) should be separated wherever possible from those responsible for its undertaking. This should ensure that:

- there is an 'outside' control on costs and resources

- a broader perspective is preserved, especially on priorities

- an external check is maintained on progress

- other interests are protected

- *'projectitus'* is avoided, ie the project team does not come to see itself as the centre of the universe

- any *'projectasaurus'* is exterminated, ie a project is terminated before it becomes so old that no-one in the organisation can recall its origins.

How to use it

Collect the proposal forms for all potential projects.

Either:

1. Rank the projects using the matrix described in more detail under the tool 'rank projects'.

Project	Benefit	Easy to do	Contribution to priority area	Total
	a	b	c	axbxc
A				
B				
C				
D				

or

2. Use Post-it® Notes to build up a priorities grid. This is described in more detail in the *Solve that problem!* Toolbox.

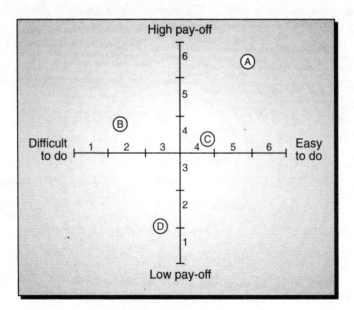

3. Develop a process improvement priority matrix to assess each project against the corporate goals:

Projects	Corporate improvement goals				
	1	2	3	4	5
1					
2					
3					

This is described in more detail in the *Solve that problem! Toolbox*.

4. Rank the projects using your chosen method.

5. Take steps to develop more detailed briefs for the highest ranking project(s).

Note. Where projects are selected by a voluntary work team that has authority to pursue its own agenda (often referred to as 'bottom-up'), it is important that the team selects a topic for improvement which:

- will have a clear benefit to customers
- requires little or no help from outside
- has a short cycle, so you can measure the effect quickly
- is not already being reviewed or changed by someone else
- is relatively simple, with clear start and end points
- is important to both team members and customers
- has a high probability of success
- is in an area where the individuals involved are likely to cooperate.

How it helps

Systematic evaluation and ranking of potential projects ensures that only those with clear benefits which contribute to corporate goals in a cost-effective manner are progressed.

THE LARGER THE RESOURCE REQUIRED FOR A PROJECT, THE MORE THOROUGH THE ORGANISATION SHOULD BE IN ITS VETTING AND SELECTION PROCEDURE

3 Set up and contract

The Setting Up Process

What it is

The process on the following page should be used to set up a project. This tool outlines each of the steps involved and clarifies who is responsible for making each happen.

How to use it

Review the process illustrated on the following page and examine each step considering the points below.

1. Make the decision to proceed

The previous tool gives three methods for deciding whether to proceed. This decision should still be provisional at this stage, subject to a preliminary assessment based on a project brief.

2. Formulate project brief

The next tool outlines how to do this.

3. Appoint team leader and key supporters

The leader should be chosen as early as possible. If there are to be a sponsor and a facilitator this is the ideal time to appoint.

4. Identify cross-functional links

Identify and consult with the areas which have an interest in the project in order to pick team members.

5. Select and appoint team members

Choose people with the right experience, skills and personal qualities to contribute to the team. Only organise the first team meeting when everyone can attend. Team roles are explained in the tool 'Clarify Roles' on page 45.

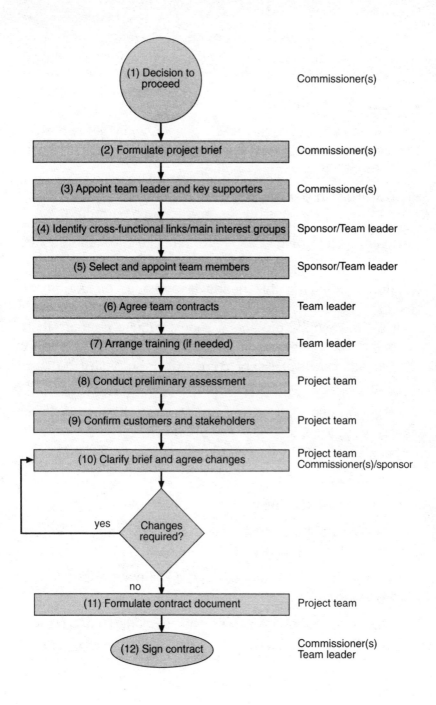

6. Agree team contracts

To cement the commitment and clarify roles a number of subsidiary contracts should be agreed. These are detailed in a separate tool.

7. Arrange training

Arrange any necessary training in technical or team skills or background briefing on the project to ensure a common approach and understanding.

8. Conduct a preliminary assessment

In order to develop a contract to which both the project team and the commissioner are committed, the team should first conduct a preliminary assessment.

How much time this needs is a matter of judgement dependent upon the complexity of the project issue. With relatively simple projects it should require no more than one or two meetings. In the case of large and complex projects, however, it should come as no surprise if the team requires several meetings spread over a few weeks.

The purpose of a preliminary assessment should be to allow the team to:

- identify principal customers and beneficiaries additional to the commissioner

- assess the feasibility of the project

- determine the principal means of achieving the project mission and primary objectives

- work out the resources which it will need and who will provide them

- recommend how far its scope and authority should extend

- formulate the best strategy for tackling the project.

9. Confirm customers and stakeholders

It is important to identify these people clearly and their needs and wants. This is covered in more detail in the tool 'Develop your project contract'.

10. Clarify brief and agree changes

The team leader should meet with the commissioner to check the brief, clarify understanding and address concerns raised by the preliminary assessment. This is likely to be an iterative process.

11. + 12. Formulate and sign the contract

This is covered in detail in later tools but the output should be a credible and commonly understood contract between the project commissioner and the project team to which both parties are fully committed.

How it helps

By following this setting up process you will ensure clarity over what you have to achieve, have the right players involved and generate commitment to the success of the project. It is time well spent.

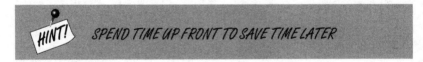

HINT! SPEND TIME UP FRONT TO SAVE TIME LATER

Develop Your Project Brief

What it is

A project brief includes the provisional definition of the problem or improvement and the project mission, objectives and terms of reference. The project commissioner uses it to brief a project team on its task.

Its purpose is to:

- sanction the establishment of a project team
- provide preliminary terms of reference from which a project contract can be derived.

A well-defined project brief should contain as a minimum, the following:

✔	Project reference number or project title
✔	Problem or improvement statement
✔	Mission and objectives
✔	Required output
✔	Scope limitations
✔	Provisional budget
✔	Provisional timescale

An ill-defined brief is likely to lead to:

✘	Inappropriate selection of project team members
✘	Vague expectations of the team
✘	Incorrect assessment of required resources and costs
✘	Scope or brief 'creep'
✘	Failure to deliver what was expected
✘	Schedule overrun

✗	Friction between the team and those outside
✗	Waste!

How to use it

1. Reflect on the project proposal.

2. Think this through in terms of:

   - What is the issue or problem it is trying to resolve?

   - What is the overall goal or mission?

   - What more specific objectives will it need to meet?

   - What specific outputs are you looking for?

   - What limits would you put around it in terms of access/money/resources/process boundaries, etc?

   - What would seem an appropriate budget?

   - Who should lead the team?

3. Use the specific tools which follow to help you answer each of these.

4. Complete a written brief for the project leader using the pro forma on the following page and advice from the next few tools.

5. Reflect on your work. Do you need to amend it? Do you need to consult with anyone at this stage?

6. Take whatever steps you need to appoint the project leader.

7. Hand over the brief to the leader to take forward.

PROJECT BRIEF	Ref No:

Title:

Issue Statement:

Mission:

Primary objectives:

Required outputs: Timing:

Scope and limits:

Budget:

Authorisation:

Cost centre:

Preliminary review and confirmation by:
Estimated project termination date:

Members   Support team

Signed: **(Commissioner)**

Date:

How it helps

It is often tempting to appoint a team and either leave it to clarify the brief or leave the brief very vague. Both of these options can lead to wasted resources, frustrated team members and few results. This tool outlines the brief which is the starting point for project clarity and focus.

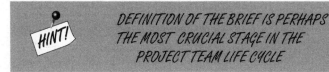

DEFINITION OF THE BRIEF IS PERHAPS THE MOST CRUCIAL STAGE IN THE PROJECT TEAM LIFE CYCLE

Write Your Issue Statement

What it is

The issue statement is a clear description of what the problem is or what needs to be improved. It is usually written by the project commissioner. There are two main types:

1. Issue statement for a problem resolution project

A problem is a deviation or departure from an existing standard. An issue statement for a project intended to resolve a problem should clearly define the standard expected and ideally the extent of the deviation.

For example:

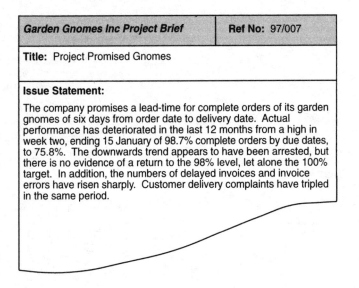

Garden Gnomes Inc Project Brief	**Ref No:** 97/007

Title: Project Promised Gnomes

Issue Statement:

The company promises a lead-time for complete orders of its garden gnomes of six days from order date to delivery date. Actual performance has deteriorated in the last 12 months from a high in week two, ending 15 January of 98.7% complete orders by due dates, to 75.8%. The downwards trend appears to have been arrested, but there is no evidence of a return to the 98% level, let alone the 100% target. In addition, the numbers of delayed invoices and invoice errors have risen sharply. Customer delivery complaints have tripled in the same period.

In the GGINC example the problem can be shown graphically, on the next page.

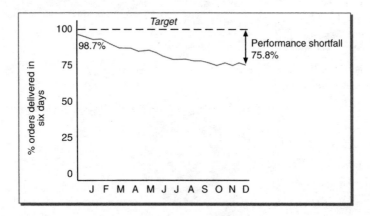

It is the cause or causes of the shortfall in performance with which the project team will be concerned.

2. Issue statements for performance elevation projects

These deal with improvements to existing performance, which may well have been previously acceptable, as distinct from departures or deviations from a standard. The circumstances in which they arise can be varied.

Examples are:

- Improve existing delivery performance in response to competitive pressure.

- Achieve a better quality product.

- Improve internal communications in response to growth in the size and complexity of the workforce.

- Reduce defects per million parts made.

- Repaint a large facility to improve its appearance.

- Relocate facilities.

- Introduce a completely new way of servicing the customer, eg direct banking.

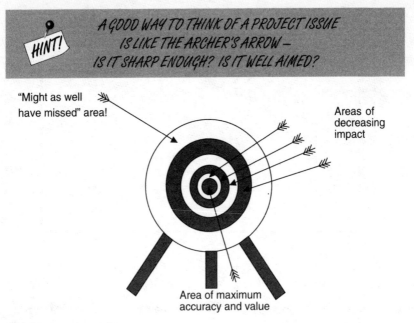

HINT!

A GOOD WAY TO THINK OF A PROJECT ISSUE
IS LIKE THE ARCHER'S ARROW –
IS IT SHARP ENOUGH? IS IT WELL AIMED?

"Might as well have missed" area!

Areas of decreasing impact

Area of maximum accuracy and value

How to use it

1. Is your goal to remedy a performance problem? If so, gather data in order to identify:

- the size of the gap between actual and required performance

- how long it has been developing/existed

- what standards/targets should apply

- any other knock-on effects.

2. Use this data to write an issue statement describing the current situation.

3. If your goal is to improve upon satisfactory performance, gather data to assess:

- why you need to improve performance

- by how much you need to improve

- how quickly you need to improve

- any knock-on implications of this change.

4. Use these ideas to write an issue statement describing how things need to change.

How it helps

An inadequately worded issue statement can lead to:

- the establishment of a project team which is not really justified
- the definition of inappropriate objectives
- the proposal of an inappropriate solution
- 'brief creep'
- schedule overrun
- limited impact on the problem.

For an issue statement to be of any value to a project team, therefore, it should be:

- *explicit* about standard and deviation
- expressed in *quantifiable* or measurable terms
- *unambiguous* in its description
- and where appropriate, clear about *trends*.

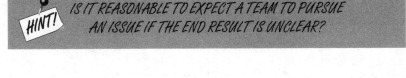

HINT! IS IT REASONABLE TO EXPECT A TEAM TO PURSUE AN ISSUE IF THE END RESULT IS UNCLEAR?

Define Your Mission and Key Objectives

What it is

The purpose of a project is described by:

- its mission or overriding goal

- the principal or primary objectives which have to be achieved if the mission is to be fulfilled

- the enabling objectives which are the means by which the primary objectives will be attained.

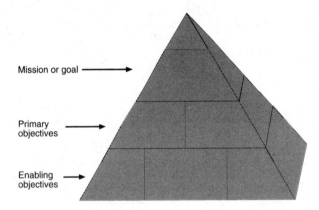

Mission or goal

Primary objectives

Enabling objectives

Thus defining the mission is vital in the evolution of a project because it:

- begins to establish if a project will have real purpose or justification

- provides the basis for defining more explicit quantified objectives

- prescribes in a general sense at least, the project's limits.

A good project mission statement will clearly:

- describe what 'it' will look like when you get there
- lift performance beyond today's level
- define the gap between today and the future
- be exciting yet feasible.

How to use it

1. Draft a mission statement for your project.

For example:

GGINC Project Brief	**Ref No:** 97/007
Title: Project Promised Gnomes	

Issue Statement:

The company promises a lead-time for complete orders of its garden gnomes of six days from order date to delivery date. Actual performance has deteriorated in the last 12 months from a high in week two, ending 15 January of 98.7% complete orders by due dates, to 75.8%. The downward trend appears to have been arrested, but there is no evidence of a return to the 98% level, let alone the 100% target. In addition, the numbers of delayed invoices and invoice errors have risen sharply. Customer delivery complaints have tripled in the same period.

Mission:

To restore GGINC to its rightful position as number one for customer deliveries – PDQ!

2. Test it against the four requirements. Is it:

- descriptive?
- uplifting?
- clear?
- feasible?

3. If not, how can you improve it?

4. To achieve your mission, you need to break it into primary objectives. These should be:

- good objectives (SMAART DUDES) – see next page
- essential to the mission
- clearly primary
- sufficient (but few) in number.

Good objectives are **SMAART DUDES**, ie they should be:

Specific	–	clear not vague
Measurable	–	change, correction or improvementshould be quantifiable
Agreed	–	between commissioner and project team
Achievable	–	attainable in the short term
Realistic	–	achievable within the period agreed
Timebound	–	defined period for achievement
Demonstrable	–	verifiable achievement
Understandable	–	comprehensible to all concerned, in particular commissioner and team should share common understanding
Deliverable	–	results capable of being delivered by the team selected
Elevated	–	outcome or result should directly contribute to a higher level goal or objective
Singular	–	one explicit end result or outcome. (More than one implies there should be more than one objective.)

Define Your Mission and Key
Objectives

For problem solving projects, the primary objective(s) should come from the principal causes of the problem, eg to train all operators to use safety equipment where the problem is a high accident level.

For performance elevation and pathfinding projects, objectives should focus on the means of achieving improved performance.

5. Draft your primary objectives.

For example:

GGINC Project Brief	Ref No: 97/007

Title: Project Promised Gnomes

Issue Statement:

The company promises a lead-time for complete orders of its garden gnomes of six days from order date to delivery date. Actual performance has deteriorated in the last 12 months from a high in week two, ending 15 January of 98.7% complete orders by due dates, to 75.8%. The downwards trend appears to have been arrested, but there is no evidence of a return to the 98% level, let alone the 100% target. In addition, the numbers of delayed invoices and invoice errors have arisen sharply. Customer delivery complaints have tripled in the same period.

Mission:

To restore GGINC to its rightful position as number one for customer deliveries – PDQ!

Primary Objectives:

(a)   100% complete and on time deliveries to agreed quality specifications within six days of order date (unless requested later by the customer)

(b)   Invoice issued within 24 hours of goods receipt, no errors

(c)   Achievement of (a) and (b) by end July.

6. Test them.

a) Ask why

    If you ask "why do we have to achieve this?" and the answer is not your mission, then there is probably something else in between which should be a primary objective.

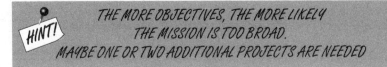

HINT!

THE MORE OBJECTIVES, THE MORE LIKELY THE MISSION IS TOO BROAD. MAYBE ONE OR TWO ADDITIONAL PROJECTS ARE NEEDED

b) Necessity

For each objective ask the question: will failure to meet this objective jeopardise or prevent achievement of the mission? If the answer is 'no', then the objective is not necessary and should be omitted.

Alternatively: what difference will it make to the mission if this objective is not met? If the answer is little or no difference, then it should be omitted.

Caution: setting the level of the objective can be all important especially in the context of the necessity test. For example: if the objective was to reduce changeover time by 60%, 40% might be absolutely essential, but anything above that desirable or even unnecessary. Thus, a 55% reduction would fail the test. The effort required to achieve that figure could be needless or wasteful.

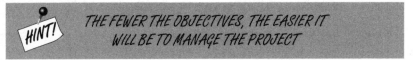

HINT! THE FEWER THE OBJECTIVES, THE EASIER IT WILL BE TO MANAGE THE PROJECT

c) Sufficiency

Question: Will meeting the primary objectives as defined be sufficient to ensure the mission is fulfilled?

Answer: 'Yes' – OK

Answer: 'No'.   Then ask: 'Why not?'

The answer should indicate either that the objectives are flawed or there is a need for additional objectives.

How it helps

Defining a clear, descriptive, lifting yet realistic Mission clarifies ultimately where a project is trying to get to. Breaking this down into a small number of SMAART DUDE objectives helps to clarify what needs to be done to achieve the Mission.

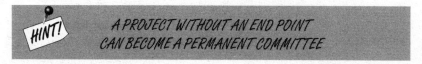

A PROJECT WITHOUT AN END POINT CAN BECOME A PERMANENT COMMITTEE

Specify Required Outputs and Timing

What it is

A project can be seen as a conversion process.

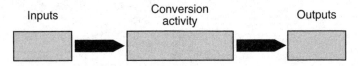

Agreeing project outputs *before* the team has started properly on its assignment:

- reduces the likelihood of misunderstandings between the project commissioner(s) and the team

- provides a basis for assessing the team's progress

- provides the means of establishing the extent to which it has fulfilled the commissioner(s) requirements.

The outputs should include:

- a plan for achieving the mission

- interim progress reports

- a measure or measures of the extent to which the objectives are being met, once the plan has been implemented

- a review or audit report, once the project has been completed. This could encompass both an evaluation of how successful the team's plan has been and a resume of lessons learnt and of course, results!

One of the key characteristics of a project is that it is timebound. A project should have a finite life, preferably the shorter the better and objectives should always be timebound. So a project brief ought to be clear on all aspects of time.

A project team should have a finite life. It makes sense, therefore, to give the best estimate of its termination date on the brief. This will:

- enable departments which are going to provide team members a chance to plan for their temporary loss or reduction of contribution

- give team members an idea of how long they are going to be involved so they can sensibly plan

- help ensure that the project commissioner and sponsor keep a close eye on how long the project is taking

- in the event of a long-term, full-time project, provide a basis for planning the re-entry of team members into the organisation.

HINT! THE LONGER THE PROJECT, THE MORE CHECKPOINTS AND MILESTONES ARE NEEDED. THE HIGHER THE CLIMB, THE MORE ROUTE CAMPS ARE NEEDED

The end point should be clearly recognisable once it has been reached.

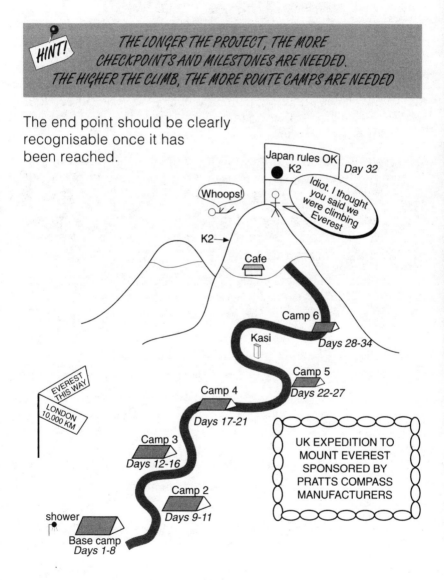

How to use it

1. Reflect on your brief. In the light of your Mission and primary objectives, what outputs will you have to produce? Complete a chart:

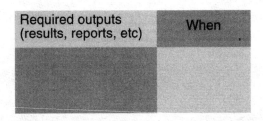

Required outputs (results, reports, etc)	When

2. How will you know if you are achieving these outputs? What measures do you need to put in place to tell you? Who will do the recording/reporting?

3. From a project management point of view, how will you know how you're doing in terms of meeting output requirements or using resources?

4. Reflect on the realism of the outputs and the timings you have identified. Are they achievable? Are they too easy?

5. If you are satisfied add them to your brief.

For example:

Project Brief	Ref No: 97/007

Title: Project Promised Gnomes

Issue statement:

The company promises a lead-time for complete orders of its garden gnomes of six days from order date to delivery date. Actual performance has deteriorated in the last 12 months from a high in week two, ending 15 January of 98.7% complete orders by due dates, to 75.8%. The downwards trend appears to have been arrested, but there is no evidence of a return to the 98% level, let alone the 100% target. In addition, the numbers of delayed invoices and invoice errors have risen sharply. Customer delivery complaints have tripled in the same period.

Mission:

To restore GGINC to its rightful position as number one for customer deliveries – PDQ!

Primary Objectives:

(a) 100% complete and on time deliveries to agreed quality specifications within six days of order date (unless requested later by the customer)
(b) Invoice issued within 24 hours of goods receipt, no errors
(c) Achievement of (a) and (b) by end July

Required Outputs:	Timing:
1. Improvement plan for approval including objectives, targets and measures.	1 March latest ending 31 July
2. Monthly progress reports.	By 8th of each month following
3. Final audit and review report.	By 30 October

How it helps

Knowing exactly what you have to produce, and when and why is a very good motivator to get down to work! By keeping focused on the agreed outputs during the project you can avoid getting sidetracked or bogged down in irrelevant or low priority tasks, or falling behind schedule.

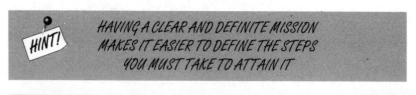

HINT!

HAVING A CLEAR AND DEFINITE MISSION MAKES IT EASIER TO DEFINE THE STEPS YOU MUST TAKE TO ATTAIN IT

Set Scope and Limits

What it is

This deals with an area that is easily overlooked when a project is being set up. To define what you expect a project to achieve is clearly necessary, but it can be just as important for the project commissioner to define what the team is not expected to encompass, or to exceed.

Hence, it is important for a project team to know the boundaries within which it should operate. Otherwise there can be confusion over the extent of its brief and the likelihood of 'scope creep' can increase. The limits can be:

- physical boundaries such as departmental, process or performance standards, product type

- budget and business plan constraints.

Limits have to be carefully judged so that they do not make the objectives unrealistic.

How to use it

1. Reflect on the mission, objectives, outputs and timing.

2. In order to achieve these:

   - who will the team need to involve? (level, functions, locations)

   - who should they exclude?

   - what performance standards or targets must they work to? (cycle times, productivity costs, etc)

   - do they need to focus geographically (eg include Europe but not US or manufacturing but not distribution centres)

   - which product areas or services are included?

- what can they not change, eg systems, vehicles, headcount, etc?
- how far can they go before referring back to the commissioner – data analysis? recommendations? implementation?

3. Write down as clearly as possible the scope and limits of the project.

An example is shown on the next page.

How it helps

Defining the scope and limits of a project helps a team to focus on what needs to be done and not to stray into other areas or waste effort on low priorities.

 CLEAR BOUNDARIES CAN LIBERATE RATHER THAN RESTRAIN PROJECT TEAMS

For example: GGINC – scope and limits

PROJECT BRIEF	Ref No: 97/007

Title: Project Promised Gnomes

Issue statement:

The company promises a lead-time for complete orders of its garden gnomes of six days from order date to delivery date. Actual performance has deteriorated in the last 12 months from a high in week two, ending 15 January of 98.7% complete orders by due dates, to 75.8%. The downwards trend appears to have been arrested, but there is no evidence of a return to the 98% level, let alone the 100% target. In addition, the numbers of delayed invoices and invoice errors have risen sharply. Customer delivery complaints have tripled in the same period.

Mission:

To restore GGINC to its rightful position as number one for customer deliveries – PDQ!

Primary objectives:

(a) 100% complete and on time deliveries to agreed quality specifications within six days of order date (unless requested later by the customer)
(b) Invoice issued within 24 hours of goods receipt, no errors
(c) Achievement of (a) and (b) by end July

Required outputs:	Timing:
1. Improvement plan for approval including objectives, targets and measures.	1 March latest ending 31 July
2. Monthly progress reports.	By 8th of each month following
3. Final audit and review report.	By 30 October

Scope and limits:

(1) Garden gnome delivery within the UK. All other products excluded.
(2) Distribution expenses to turnover target for this year not to be exceeded
(3) This year's distribution operating expense budget not to be exceeded.

Agree Project Budget

What it is

Depending upon the type of project the budget can vary from a few hundred to millions of pounds. The project team should be aware from the outset of the budget within which it has to operate and of the control system which it should observe.

If it is intended that normal expenditure procedures should apply, then this should be stipulated together with an appropriate cost centre.

If, however, an extraordinary or special system of expenditure and cost control is required then details should be attached to the brief.

How it is done

1. Reflect on the objectives and scope of the project.

2. Think about the costs involved in undertaking the project. Identify the main categories, for example:

- Manpower (salaries, benefits and taxes).
- Materials (raw materials, etc).
- Equipment (machines, tools, hardware, telecommunications etc).
- Premises (space, heat, facilities, etc).
- Expenses (travel, accommodation, allowances, etc).
- Subcontractors (designers, consultants, manufacturers, lawyers, etc).
- Reorganisation costs (redundant stock, closures, headcount reductions, etc).

3. Estimate the weekly costs of each over the life of the project.

4. If the project is likely to go on for some time it may be necessary to spread costs over time (particularly across financial years).

5. It may also be necessary to depreciate capital costs. Seek financial advice on this.

6. Prepare a budget statement for the project showing in round terms costs (and incidental income) through the life of the project.

7. Avoid being too detailed – at this stage it is very difficult to be accurate.

8. If the benefits of the project have not already been quantified, it is important to do so now so that the project can be cost justified. In calculating benefits take into account increased sales, improved margins, better customer retention, increased productivity, etc.

9. Add the proposed budget to the project brief.

10. Clarify authorisation levels and cost centre(s).

How it helps

Almost any problem can be resolved or situation improved by throwing money at it. Realistically, however, there are always limits. A project team should be aware of and empowered to manage its budget to achieve the best possible results within the agreed financial constraints.

HINT! NOTHING COMES FOR FREE AND THAT INCLUDES GOING AFTER GOOD IDEAS, IMPROVEMENTS OR PROBLEMS

Clarify Roles

What it is

Having the right people involved is key to the success of a project team. Without all the relevant knowledge, skills and experience and, above all, the enthusiasm and will to succeed, it will be extremely difficult to produce quality results.

The most fundamental relationship is that of commissioner and project leader. A person, or an entity such as a company Board, is commissioning a 'contractor' (the leader) to undertake an assignment –the 'project'.

Another way of viewing this relationship is as 'customer' and 'supplier'. However, the commissioner may not be the only customer and then not necessarily the most important one.

Even a simple project undertaken by one person can involve a complex web of relationships and roles. This is certainly the case when a project is being undertaken by a team of people.

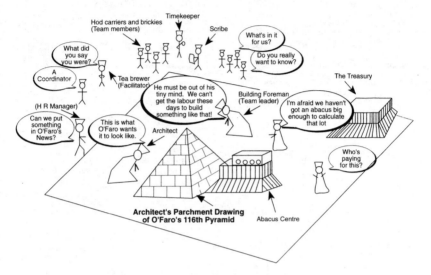

Architect's Parchment Drawing of O'Faro's 116th Pyramid

There are both formal and informal roles within and around a team and different types of relationships which develop from them.

There are five key roles involved.

1. *Commissioner* – person or committee responsible for authorising the project.

2. *Sponsor* – who actively supports the team from 'outside', secures resources, clears the pathway and ensures the team is 'hooked' into the organisation.

[*Note*: the sponsor and commissioner can be one and the same depending on the size, importance and complexity of the project.]

3. *Team leader* – who leads the improvement team.

4. *Facilitator* – who provides practical guidance and support to the sponsor, leader and team members on how to operate effectively.

5. *Team members* – who carry out projects and implement improvements.

[*Note*: Other roles which might be applicable in large multi-team projects, such as the project manager, are not considered here.]

Commissioner

This is either a person or a body, like a management committee or company Board. The easiest way to view the role of the commissioner is that he/she/they is/are the immediate customer/s of the project team.

There may be other customers who stand to benefit from a project team's output and indeed the commissioner may not be the main immediate beneficiary of that output. However, the immediate customer is the commissioner, because he, she or it:

- *authorises* the setting up of the project team

- *defines* the preliminary *brief*

- *approves* the team's terms of reference, which are defined in a project contract

- eventually *approves* its recommendations and implementation plans.

Sponsor

The sponsor role ensures that the project team has the support of senior line management. The role of the sponsor is to:

- provide a link to senior line management and company wide activity

- secure the necessary resources for the team

- support, show active interest in, but not lead the project
- if also the commissioner, approve (but not dictate) the project contract
- provide approval for implementing solutions, or to provide guidance on the approval process.

Once an improvement team has developed its solutions and is ready to implement its action plan, the team will be in one of two situations.

1. The responsibility and authority to implement the action plan lies with the team members, in which case they move straight ahead with implementation.

2. Approval is needed from a higher authority, ie the project commissioner(s) to implement the recommended changes.

It is the sponsor's responsibility to ensure that:

- the team leader is clearly aware of the approval process
- the appropriate approvals are given
- this is done in a timely fashion. There is nothing worse for a project team than waiting for weeks to hear if their recommended solutions have been accepted or not.

Team leader

The role of the team leader is to:

- manage the project team and its activities
- clarify and modify (by agreement with the commissioner) the mission and objectives
- liaise with the team sponsor to agree plans and discuss issues
- enrol appropriate partners (customers or suppliers)
- negotiate for, procure and allocate resources to the project (with the sponsor)

- tackle functional barriers, resolve functional conflicts
- create commitment to, and ownership of, the mission and objectives amongst the team
- empower project team members to identify and, where authorised, to implement improvements
- drive and stimulate improvements
- provide reports to the project commissioner(s) and local management.

Team leaders can be asked to lead projects because they:

- manage the particular process or area to be improved
- have experience of leading teams
- are enthusiastic champions
- will benefit from the experience of leading a team
- bring a fresh pair of eyes to the topic to be addressed.

Project team leaders need not be managers and may not have had previous experience of leading a team.

Team members

Team members will be involved in the project team either because:

- they are part of the process which is being improved, or
- they are customers/suppliers of the process, or
- they want to be involved and are enthusiastic.

> **HINT!** TEAM MEMBERS SHOULD HAVE A STAKE IN THE OUTCOME OF THE PROJECT – THEY ARE THEN MORE LIKELY TO BE COMMITTED

Team members need to:

- see team membership as part of their job and not an intrusion

- contribute during meetings:
  - sharing knowledge and experience
  - using skills
  - listening and asking questions
  - helping others to participate
- carry out tasks between meetings, such as:
  - data gathering
  - testing solutions
  - measuring improvements
- take joint ownership and therefore share responsibility for the effectiveness of the team.

Team members may change during the course of a project to reflect the changing needs of the task and the commitments of the team members.

Facilitator

The role of the facilitator in supporting an improvement team is to:

- provide guidance/support to the leader, sponsor and if appropriate, team members
- facilitate the improvement process
- be fixers and inspirers
- identify and help remove blockages.

Once the facilitator has been enlisted it is up to the team leader and the facilitator to agree how much involvement/support from the facilitator is required. Facilitators may not need to attend all team meetings, but will work with the team leader either before or after a meeting to ensure success.

Facilitators can work with team leaders to:

- develop a plan of how to approach the project
- test ideas
- give feedback on plans and performance

- advise on the use of tools and techniques

- attend meetings to help with the process or observe performance

- review progress and identify improvements in any way which facilitates progress!

How to use it

1. As soon as it is decided to progress a project, the commissioner should be identified. Particularly if it is a team role, it is helpful to identify a specific individual to be sponsor to the project team. This is also done where the commissioner is very senior and unable to get involved to any extent in specific projects.

2. Once the commissioner or sponsor has developed a draft brief, the team leader should be identified.

3. As soon as the commissioner/sponsor/leader have agreed roles and approached interested functions, the process of identifying and agreeing team members can begin.

4. It is helpful to decide early whether to involve a facilitator. If the decision is to do so there is merit in using someone from an unrelated functional area so it is clear their role is to focus on the process of setting up the team, using tools, running meetings, etc and not the functional content of their project.

5. Once identified all players should spend some time agreeing personal contracts prior to the first team meeting (see later tool).

6. If the project links to others, strengthen these links through roles. For example: in the case of a top-down project team, the commissioners of a sub-project team can be the main project team and so on. Ideally, either the sponsor or the team leader of a sub-project team should be drawn from the commissioning team to ensure a good communication link between the teams.

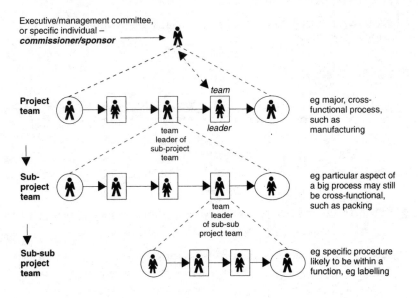

Executive/management committee, or specific individual – **commissioner/sponsor**

Project team — *team leader* — eg major, cross-functional process, such as manufacturing

team leader of sub-project team

Sub-project team — eg particular aspect of a big process may still be cross-functional, such as packing

team leader of sub-sub project team

Sub-sub project team — eg specific procedure likely to be within a function, eg labelling

7. You can now complete the project brief:

PROJECT BRIEF: *GGINC*	Ref No: 97/007

Title: Project Promised Gnomes

Issue statement:

The Company promises a lead-time for complete orders of its garden gnomes of six days from order receipt to delivery date. Actual performance has deteriorated in the last 12 months from a high in week 2, ending 15 January of 98.7% complete orders by due dates, to 75.8%. The downwards trend appears to have been arrested, but there is no evidence of a return to the 98% level, let alone the 100% target. In addition, the numbers of delayed invoices and invoice errors have risen sharply. Customer delivery complaints have tripled in the same period.

Mission:

To restore GGINC to its rightful position as number one for customer deliveries – PDQ!

Primary objectives:

(a) 100% complete and on time order deliveries to agreed quality specifications within six days of order date (unless requested later by the customer)

(b) Invoice issued within 24 hours of goods receipt, no errors

(c) Achievement of (a) and (b) by end July.

Required outputs:

(1) Improvement plan for approval including objectives, targets and measures

(2) Monthly progress reports

(3) Final audit and review report

Timing:

1 March latest ending 31 July

(by 8th of each month following

(by 30 October

Scope and limits:

(1) Garden gnomes delivery within the UK. All other products excluded

(2) Distribution expenses to turnover target for this year not to be exceeded

(3) This year's distribution operating expense budget not to be exceeded

Budget: provisional £55,000 contingency below distribution operating expenses line

Authorisation required: normal procedures with sponsor authority

Cost centre: 97/OPI

Preliminary review and confirmation: by 21 January

Estimated project termination date: 1 November

Members

(1) Leader: S C D Stiff, Systems Manager

(2) Members: To be appointed by 8 January after discussion between I T Fright and S C D Stiff

Support team

(1) Sponsor: I T Fright, Distribution Director

Facilitator: E Z Going, Quality Control Analyst

Signed: for and on behalf of GGINC Steering Group:
Date: 20 December

How it helps

Getting the right players involved in clearly defined roles ensures the necessary experience, skills and personal qualities are available to the project. Without these, the project is unlikely to succeed.

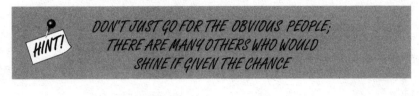

HINT!

DON'T JUST GO FOR THE OBVIOUS PEOPLE; THERE ARE MANY OTHERS WHO WOULD SHINE IF GIVEN THE CHANCE

Develop Personal Contracts

What they are

Contracts clarify what is expected and who is doing what. This tool gives checklists to use to structure discussions between the various parties in order to agree role contracts.

How to use it

1. Identify which contract you wish to establish.

2. Refer to the relevant checklist.

3. Arrange a short meeting to discuss roles.

4. Use the checklist as an agenda.

5. Follow up any outstanding points or actions.

6. Make a note of what you have agreed for future review.

7. Refer to *Build that team!* Toolbox for more detailed guidance onhandlingmeetings/building teams, etc.

Checklist for initial contracting meeting between project commissioner/sponsor and team leader

✔ Is it clear who is involved?

- • Does the team leader feel comfortable about leading this team?

- • If already chosen, are the team members appropriate? (The right balance of technical and personal roles)

- • Who else should be involved? (In perhaps a special advisor capacity)

✔ Is the project brief clear enough to begin a preliminary assessment?

- • Is the problem or opportunity for improvement too big for this team to handle?

- • What is the timeframe for completion of the preliminary assessment?

- • How will you know when the problem is solved?

- • What are the progress reporting requirements to commissioner/sponsor – frequency, method?

✔ How will the project commissioner and/or sponsor show interest/be involved in the teams activities?

- • Attendance at team meetings – when, how many, for what duration?

- • Recognition for effort/during the project/when result achieved?

✔ What resistance is anticipated to the team working on this improvement opportunity (if any)? How should it be handled?

✔ What reservations (if any) does the team leader have about this project or the team?

✔ Has the team leader had an initial meeting with the facilitator? If not, schedule it as soon as possible

✔ What are the next steps?

Checklist for initial contracting meeting between team leader and facilitator

✔ Roles

- Project sponsor/commissioner – has any discussion taken place?
- Facilitator – now and ongoing?
- Team leader?
- Team members – are they the right people/who should they be?

✔ Clarity of project brief – has it been agreed with project sponsor?

✔ Possible team ground rules

✔ Meetings management generally:

- Timing
- Use of agenda and minutes
- Meeting review

✔ First meeting venue/materials (flipchart, storyboard etc)

✔ Team leader skills

- Building the team
- Handling difficult situations

✔ Need for team-building exercise(s) – introductions, icebreakers, practice in using tools

✔ Level of understanding/exposure of the team – establish whether need exists to spend time on revisiting principles, or tools and techniques, in early meetings

✔ Learning points from involvement in other projects

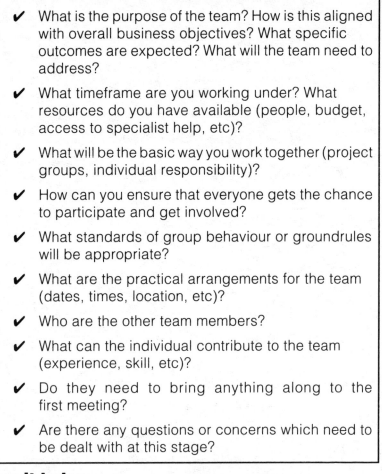

Checklist for initial contracting meeting between team leader and team members

✔ What is the purpose of the team? How is this aligned with overall business objectives? What specific outcomes are expected? What will the team need to address?

✔ What timeframe are you working under? What resources do you have available (people, budget, access to specialist help, etc)?

✔ What will be the basic way you work together (project groups, individual responsibility)?

✔ How can you ensure that everyone gets the chance to participate and get involved?

✔ What standards of group behaviour or groundrules will be appropriate?

✔ What are the practical arrangements for the team (dates, times, location, etc)?

✔ Who are the other team members?

✔ What can the individual contribute to the team (experience, skill, etc)?

✔ Do they need to bring anything along to the first meeting?

✔ Are there any questions or concerns which need to be dealt with at this stage?

How it helps

It is easier to perform well when you know what is expected of you. This tool will help all of the parties in a project to define their roles and reach agreement with each other on how to work together before embarking on the 'meat' of the project.

Develop Your Project Contract

What it is

Definition

A project contract is an *agreement* between a project team

- the supplier – and the project commissioner(s) or sponsor
- the customer, to meet defined objectives in order to fulfil a mission which relates to a specific problem or improvement.

The project contract is derived from the project brief and should reflect the project team's own views on the task it has been set; in particular, the objectives which must be met if the mission is to be achieved.

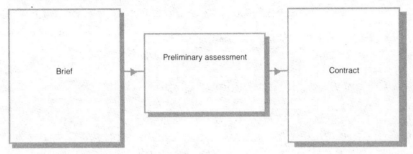

How to use it

1. Identify the stakeholders in the project.

Start with the project's principal customers. These will be:

- the person or group commissioning the project
- those who stand to gain from its success in terms of needs or wants being satisfied
- those who can be expected to use its results.

There will be others who:

- will not benefit from the project's results, but are expected to contribute significantly.

- might suffer/lose significantly as a consequence of the project, eg through reorganisation.

All of these should be consulted on the project brief before a contract is drawn up.

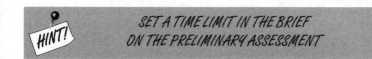

HINT!

SET A TIME LIMIT IN THE BRIEF
ON THE PRELIMINARY ASSESSMENT

2. Decide what you need to know from them and develop a checklist. For example:

- Do they think this project should be done (now)?
- Are they satisfied with the description of the problem?
- Are the mission/goals/measures OK?
- How will they judge your success?
- How will their department be affected?
- Do they have any concerns?

3. Try to interview rather than send a questionnaire – you have a better chance of exploring concerns or ideas.

4. Analyse the responses to:

- identify changes to the brief
- gauge likely resistance
- highlight things to include in your contract.

5. Start to draft your contract. Refer to other specific tools for help to do this.

For example:

PROJECT CONTRACT: Project Promised Gnomes	Ref No: 97/007

Issue statement:

The Company promises a lead-time for complete orders of its garden gnomes of 6 days from order receipt to delivery date. Actual performance has deteriorated in the last 12 months from a high in week 2, ending 15 January of 98.7% complete orders by due dates, to 75.8%. The downwards trend appears to have been arrested, but there is no evidence of a return to the 98% level, let alone the 100% target. In addition, the numbers of delayed invoices and invoice errors have risen sharply. Customer delivery complaints have tripled in the same period.

Mission:

Number one for customer deliveries – 'PDQ'.

Principal customers	Team	Members:	Supporters	Facilitator:
Commissioner(s)	Leader:	C O Ventry	Sponsor:	E Z Going
Stew I T Upham	S C D Stiff	W A Saul	I T Fright	
		L E Stir		
Other:		A Villa		
Sales		S Sitay		

Scope and limits:
(1) Garden gnomes delivery within the UK. All other products excluded
(2) Distribution expenses to turnover target for this year not to be exceeded
(3) This year's distribution operating expense budget not to be exceeded

Authority to:
(a) N/A
(b) N/A
(c) Set up no more than 2 sub-project teams
(d) Recommend, implement after approval and adjust

Required outputs:
(1) Improvement plan for approval including objectives, targets and measures
(2) Monthly progress reports
(3) Final audit and review report

Rspy	Dates
(1) Team	(1) 1 April
(2) SCD Stiff	(2) by 8th each month
(3) Team & auditor	(3) 30 November

Budget	Authorisation required	Planned termination date
Provisional £55,000 contingency below distribution operating expenses line	Normal procedure, sponsor authority **Cost centre:** 95/OPI	31 December

Signatories:

S. Upham III	S.C.D. Stiff	I.T. Fright
Commissioner	Team leader	Sponsor
Date: 19 January	Date: 18 January	Date: 18 January

Note: objectives and measures overleaf.

Primary objectives	Key measures	Milestones By 31.3	By 31.5	By 31.7	Principal means	Measures	Objectives
1. Sustainable minimum of 98% complete and on time deliveries within six days by 30 September	1.1. Proportion of orders delivered complete by due date (W)	>80%	>90%	>98%	1.1. Reduce secondary product range 1.2. Reduce manufacturing cycle time for top 12 products (80% output) 1.3. Improve stock accuracy	1.1. Proportion of secondary products manufactured in-house 1.2. Length of lead times in days for each of the top 12 products 1.3. Book to physical stock comparison – number of separate stock item discrepancies – reasons for discrepancies 1.4. To be developed in relation to appropriate strategies	1.1. 50% reduction in secondary products manufactured in house, by 31 August 1.2. Minimum 30% reduction in top 12 products unexpecting lead times by 31 July 1.3. Minimum 98% stock accuracy by 30 June 1.4. Implement stategy for tackling other stock-out root causes by 30 April
2. All customers invoiced 100% accurately within 24 hours of goods receipt	2.1. Percentage of invoices sent within 24 hours of order receipt by customer (W, M) 2.2. Percentage of invoices with errors (W, M)	2.1 >90% 2.2 <5%	>95% <3%	>100% 0	2.1. Issue invoice with goals delivery note and/or fax same day 2.2. Track causes of errors and institute corrective action	2.1. Percentage of invoices sent with orders (W, M) 2.2. To be determined	2.1. 100% invoices sent with orders 2.2. Zero errors

* Frequency of measure: W = weekly, M=monthly, Q = quarterly

6. Check out things on the project brief which you feel are unclear.

7. Be prepared to suggest modifications to the brief if you really feel uncomfortable about it. However, try to focus on how you will achieve the brief.

8. Develop the 'Authorities' section of the contract. Will you be:

   - recommending?

   - implementing?

   - setting up sub project teams?

   - amending?

   Clearly the definition of 'Authorities' will impact on the outputs you have to deliver.

9. Start work on how you will achieve your primary objectives. This involves identifying the principal **means**. The bigger and more complex the project, the more difficult it will be to assess these quickly.

10. Once you have identified the broad **means** you can go on to set specific measures and enabling objectives which relate to them. These clarify what you will have to do to achieve your primary objectives.

11. When the contract is finished and agreed by all partners, it should be signed to demonstrate commitment and understanding.

FUNCTIONAL INTERESTS OFTEN OVERLAP – BUT DO NOT EXPECT THE SAME DEGREE OF COMMITMENT FROM EACH FUNCTION OR DEPARTMENT

How it helps

Contracting is a process which helps to ensure the project brief is appropriate but more significantly it:

* generates ownership of the means or the 'how'
* encourages the team to feel a genuine party to the contract.

GOOD FOUNDATIONS PRODUCE SOLID RESULTS

4 Plan what to do

Use a Project Management Plan

What it is

During the life of a project there are two types of plan.

- Plan for managing a project or *project management plan.* This outlines the steps or process that the project will go through, who is involved and when.

- Plan for implementing the solution(s) or *implementation plan.* This is usually far more complex and can only be developed as the project unfolds.

Project management plan

This sets out the five main phases in the life of a project and their key steps, with scheduled completion dates and assigned responsibilities.

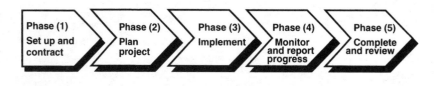

One way of describing it is as the 'administrative' or 'management' plan of a project.

It summarises what must be completed:

- by when and
- by whom

in terms of the management or administrative process.

The initial plan is often drafted by the commissioner but responsibility passes to the team leader once in place. So while this tool is described at this stage in the Toolbox, in reality it will have existed in some form from the moment the project was identified.

The project management plan should also cover such issues as:

- whether or not to use subcontractors
- whether the team is full or part-time
- whether objectives should be tackled in parallel or series.

The implementation plan is dealt with in the next tool.

How to use it

1. Use the pro forma on the next page to plan Phase 1 (Setting up) of your project.

2. Identify the steps which have to be undertaken in Phases 2-5 of your specific project.

3. Develop and complete pro formas for these phases showing start and completion dates, who will be responsible and the current status.

PROJECT MANAGEMENT PLAN SAMPLE LAYOUT				
Project (Title)			Ref No:	
Project Step	Start by	Complete by	Prime responsibility	Status
Phase 1				
1.1 Decision to proceed				
1.2 Develop preliminary brief				
1.3 Support team leader				
1.4 Identify cross-functional links/main interest groups				
1.5 Select team members				
1.6 Train team				
1.7 Conclude team contracts				
1.8 Do preliminary assessment				
1.9 Confirm customers and stakeholders				
1.10 Clarify brief and agree changes				
1.11 Formulate contract document				
1.12 Sign contract				
Phase 2				

How it helps

A project management plan outlines what has to be done by whom in order to get a project up and running and operating successfully.

HINT!

FAILURE TO PLAN CAN MEAN
PLANNING TO FAIL

Decide What To Do

What it is

Although this is only one tool in this Toolbox, it is the very heart of your project as it encompasses steps 4 - 6 of the Plan–Do–Check–Act improvement process, namely:

- collect data
- analyse (for root causes)
- find solutions.

These three steps are outlined briefly here and cross-referenced with a selection of tools which are described fully in the *Solve that problem!* Toolbox.

The way in which you tackle the steps will vary depending on the nature of your project. If your job is to tackle a problem in an existing process, your focus will be different to the one you would use for tackling a completely new situation such as setting up a green field site.

How to use it

1. Collect data

This step involves collecting information on what happens today. It can include:

- mapping the current process
- surveying customers operator/suppliers, etc
- monitoring performance standards
- measuring waste/rework errors, etc

Possible tools to use

Check Sheets
Data Display
Process Mapping
Time-Cost Analysis

- assessing efficiency or productivity.

Without this data it is very difficult to objectively assess the scale of improvement needed. It also can provide useful clues on root causes and potential solutions.

2. Analyse for root causes or critical improvement factors

Without adequate data it may prove difficult to identify the real (root) causes of your problem. This step may prove frustrating without having collected all of the relevant data under the previous step. When dealing with an improvement in performance which is satisfactory today, but will need to change, you will be looking for critical improvement factors.

Asking Why
Brainstorming
Cause and Effect Analysis
Paired Comparisons
Pareto Analysis
Process Mapping
Process Improvement
Priorities Grid
Time-Cost Analysis

3. Find the best solution

By now the team should be in possession of all the relevant information surrounding the cause and effect of this particular improvement op-portunity. It can then go on to solve the problem. A key part of this step is choosing and applying the criteria to help in selecting the best solution; a solution that just looks or feels good may not be good enough – the team must prove its value.

Brainstorming
Consensus Reaching
Cost Benefit Analysis
Paired Comparisons
Decision Chart
Priorities Grid

How it helps

By systematically understanding what is happening today and why; and then creatively identifying future options you are well positioned to develop innovative, workable solutions.

Develop Implementation Plans

What they are

Once you have decided on your solution to the problem or issue at the heart of your project, you are ready to develop a plan to implement it.

An implementation plan should contain or identify:

- the key tasks which will have to be undertaken to achieve the enabling objective(s)

- the owner(s) or person(s) responsible for completing each task

- their sequence, duration and timing

- resources required

- costs

- contingency steps.

It would be difficult to incorporate all of this information in one easy to use document. For this reason an implementation plan should normally comprise the following:

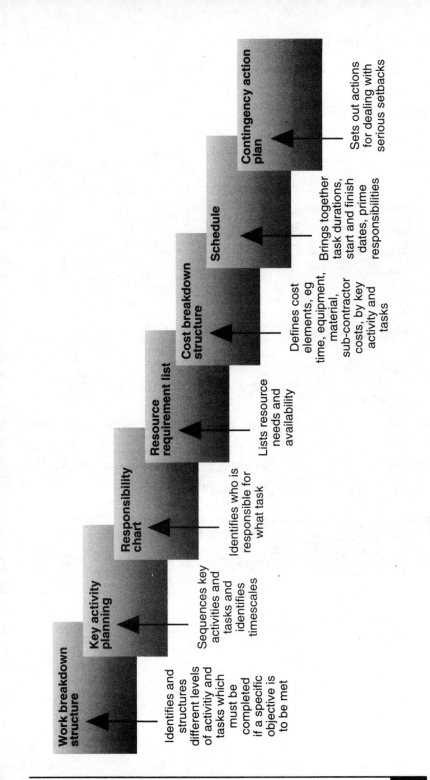

Work breakdown structure — Identifies and structures different levels of activity and tasks which must be completed if a specific objective is to be met

Key activity planning — Sequences key activities and tasks and identifies timescales

Responsibility chart — Identifies who is responsible for what task

Resource requirement list — Lists resource needs and availability

Cost breakdown structure — Defines cost elements, eg time, equipment, material, sub-contractor costs, by key activity and tasks

Schedule — Brings together task durations, start and finish dates, prime responsibilities

Contingency action plan — Sets out actions for dealing with serious setbacks

How to use it

1. Read through the various planning charts that are included in this section of the Toolbox.

2. As you read, decide whether each is needed for the specific project you are about to start.

Tools	Needed? ✓	Not needed? ✗
Work breakdown structure		
Cost breakdown structure		
Key activity and task plans		
Responsibility chart		
Resource requirement list		
Schedule		
Contingency Action Plan		

3. Develop appropriate pro formas to use based on the examples given for each tool.

4. Follow the planning process using the tools (see next page).

5. Follow the detailed instructions on 'How to use it' for each tool, using this Toolbox and also the *Solve that problem!* Toolbox.

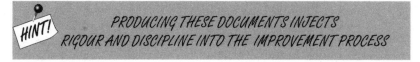

HINT!

PRODUCING THESE DOCUMENTS INJECTS RIGOUR AND DISCIPLINE INTO THE IMPROVEMENT PROCESS

The planning process

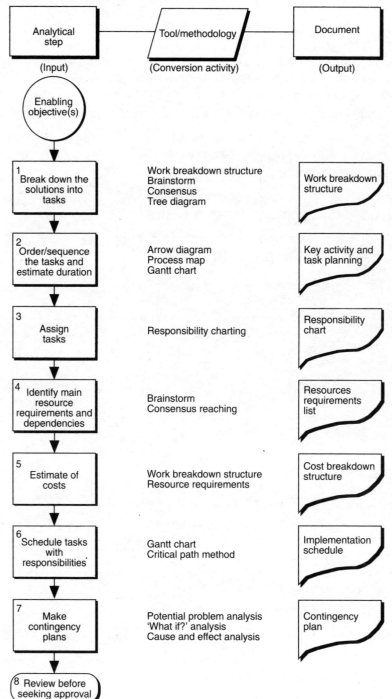

Analytical step	Tool/methodology	Document
(Input)	(Conversion activity)	(Output)

Enabling objective(s)

Analytical step	Tool/methodology	Document
1 Break down the solutions into tasks	Work breakdown structure Brainstorm Consensus Tree diagram	Work breakdown structure
2 Order/sequence the tasks and estimate duration	Arrow diagram Process map Gantt chart	Key activity and task planning
3 Assign tasks	Responsibility charting	Responsibility chart
4 Identify main resource requirements and dependencies	Brainstorm Consensus reaching	Resources requirements list
5 Estimate of costs	Work breakdown structure Resource requirements	Cost breakdown structure
6 Schedule tasks with responsibilities	Gantt chart Critical path method	Implementation schedule
7 Make contingency plans	Potential problem analysis 'What if?' analysis Cause and effect analysis	Contingency plan

8 Review before seeking approval

How it helps

Plans help you use resources efficiently and effectively. They dramatically increase your chances of success and greatly reduce the stress levels of those involved. Plans are therefore essential ingredients in making things happen.

The implementation plan is made up of several different documents which together clarify exactly what has to be done when, by whom, with what.

How many of the documents you need will depend on the nature and complexity of your project.

The following tools will help you to prepare the necessary elements of your implementation plan.

Develop Implementation Plans: Work Breakdown Structure

What it is

A Work Breakdown Structure (WBS) is used to identify the tasks which must be completed if an objective or result is to be achieved. (Sometimes referred to as a top-down flow chart.)

WBS involves systematically breaking down an objective until very specific tasks are identified.

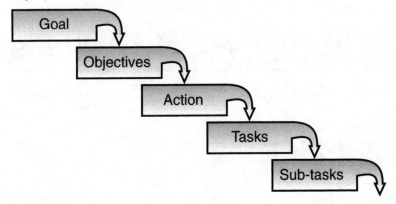

How to use it

1. First define the goal you want to achieve.

2. Then identify the main means by which the goal is to be met. The required outcomes of each of these can be expressed in the form of enabling objectives or results.

    NB: steps 1+2 should already have been done as part of the project brief.

3. List the key actions which must be taken to achieve each enabling objective.

4. For each key action identify the tasks which must be completed.

5. For a task which is sizeable or relatively complex, identify the sub-tasks.

6. Set out the breakdown analysis by using one of the two formats, whichever is most suitable: hierarchy or list. The example shows both formats.

For example: painting the house: hierarchical format:

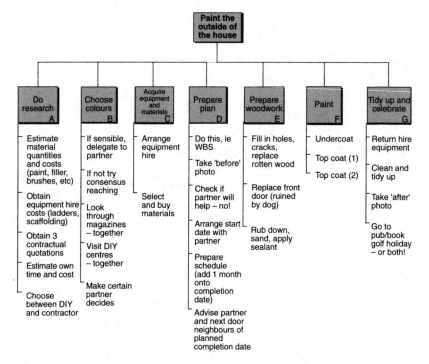

For example: painting the house list format:

A. Do research

1. Estimate material quantities and costs (paint, filler, brushes, etc).

2. Obtain equipment hire costs (ladders, scaffolding).

3. Obtain three contractual quotations.

4. Estimate own time and cost.

5. Choose between DIY and contractor.

B. Choose colour

1. If sensible, delegate to partner.
2. If not, try consensus reaching.
3. Look through magazines – together.
4. Visit DIY centres – together.
5. Make certain partner decides.

C. Obtain equipment and materials

1. Agree equipment hire.
2. Select and buy materials.

D. Prepare implementation plan

1. Do this, ie WBS.
2. Take 'before' photo.
3. Check if partner will help – no!
4. Arrange start date with partner.
5. Prepare schedule (add one month onto completion date).
6. Advise partner and next door neighbours of planned completion date.

E. Undertake preliminary preparation

1. Fill in holes, cracks replace rotten wood.
2. Replace front door (ruined by dog).
3. Rub down, sand, apply sealant.

F. Apply paint

1. Undercoat.
2. Top coat (one).
3. Top coat (two).

G. Tidy up and celebrate

1. Return hire equipment.

2. Clean and tidy up.

3. Take 'after' photo.

4. Go to pub/book golf holiday – or both!

There are certain guidelines for producing a WBS.

1. Only people who know the work should produce a WBS.

2. A WBS can be produced as a whole by a team working together. An alternative approach is to agree the headings; then assign each to one or two people who best know what would be involved and can therefore judge more accurately the level down to which the constituent WBS should be taken.

3. The level of detail to which each arm of a WBS should be analysed will vary according to need.

4. The level of detail to which you should take a WBS should be determined by the level of accuracy and exactness needed, eg to produce a detailed schedule, or roughly estimate resource requirements.

5. A WBS is a preliminary step to producing a schedule and resources estimate. Thus, the timing and ordering of actions or details of responsibilities and man hours involved are not the concern at this stage. The WBS is an aid to defining these requirements simply by listing the main actions or tasks.

How it helps

WBS is a structured way of identifying and presenting the different levels of tasks and activities which must be undertaken to achieve a specific objective or output.

Develop Implementation Plans: Key Activity and Task Plans

What it is

It is useful to plan at two levels: key activities and tasks.

- **Key activity planning**

  Key activities are the 'milestones' for a project. They are the main steps along the results path of an objective. Key activity planning is done with the project team using flipcharts and Post-it® Notes so that a number of variations can be tried easily until a final plan is agreed.

- **Task planning**

  Task planning is concerned with identifying the specific tasks required to achieve a key activity. They are not prepared for each key activity on the key activity plan all at once. Rather a rolling approach is more appropriate, ie only planning tasks for key activities to be reached in the next few weeks (shorter projects) or months (longer projects) to replace plans for key activities currently being reached.

How to use it

1. Identify the key tasks required to achieve a key activity (may be available from WBS).

2. Sequence the tasks using flowcharting (see Process Mapping in the *Solve that problem!* Toolbox).

3. Identify the people involved in the tasks and their roles and responsibilities (Responsibilities Chart).

4. Estimate the work content of each task for each person. (Use actual historic data on task duration if this is available).

5. Schedule the tasks.

For example: Key activity planning

Date of plan preparation	Project title: Company/organisation:	Office Relocation, Lakeside Business Park ACME Accountants Ltd

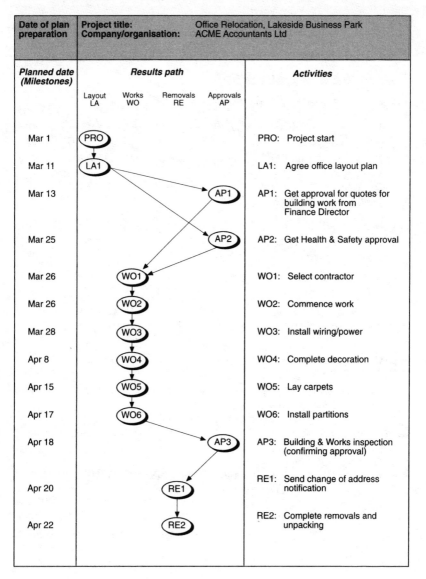

Planned date (Milestones)	Results path	Activities
	Layout LA — Works WO — Removals RE — Approvals AP	
Mar 1	PRO	PRO: Project start
Mar 11	LA1	LA1: Agree office layout plan
Mar 13	AP1	AP1: Get approval for quotes for building work from Finance Director
Mar 25	AP2	AP2: Get Health & Safety approval
Mar 26	WO1	WO1: Select contractor
Mar 26	WO2	WO2: Commence work
Mar 28	WO3	WO3: Install wiring/power
Apr 8	WO4	WO4: Complete decoration
Apr 15	WO5	WO5: Lay carpets
Apr 17	WO6	WO6: Install partitions
Apr 18	AP3	AP3: Building & Works inspection (confirming approval)
Apr 20	RE1	RE1: Send change of address notification
Apr 22	RE2	RE2: Complete removals and unpacking

For example: Task schedule

Task schedule *(worked example)*													
Project: Office relocation		**Key activity no./name:** LA1 – Office layout											
Schedule issue date:		**Approved by:** Estates manager											
Prepared by: Estates officer		**Key activity target completion date:** 11 March											
Task name	*Total est.work content (days)*	*Period (days) Gantt chart*											
		M1	2	3	4	5	6	7	8	9	10	11	
1. Hold meeting with staff	0.25	⊢											
2. Meeting with staff and designer (develop specification)	0.5	⊢											
			⊢――――――――⊣										
3. Designer produces options	4.0						⊢						
4. Meeting with staff and designer to agree layout option	0.25								⊢――――――――⊣				
5. Preparation of production drawings for costing and H&S approval	5.0												

How it helps

Key activity and task plans identify exactly what has to be done
and when. They are the key to actually making things happen
in an organised and controlled way.

Develop Implementation Plans: Responsibility Chart

What it is

A responsibility chart identifies and assigns team members and others to the tasks to be done.

How to use it

1. Discuss with the team what has to be done and agree who is best placed to do each task.

2. Develop responsibility labels or codes to further clarify role and level of action required against the key activities and tasks in which people are involved. For example:

   P = prime responsibility

   W = does the work

   I = has input

   A = advises

   D = takes decision

   C = must be consulted

   IF = must be informed.

3. Add this information to the task schedule. An example is shown on the next page.

How it helps

The responsibility chart adds the vital dimension of 'who' to the task schedule. It helps each team member to plan, monitor and review their contribution to the project and enables the leader to track how the team is being deployed.

Responsibility chart

Key: P = prime responsibility
W = does the work
I = has input
A = advises
D = takes decision
C = must be consulted
IF = must be informed

Task schedule

Project:	Office relocation		Key activity no/name: LA1 – Office layout
Schedule issue date:			Approved by:
Prepared by:	Estates officer		Key activity target completion date: 11 March

Task name	Total est. work content (days)	M1	2	3	4	5	6	7	8	9	10	11	Est. mgr	Est. officer	Est. PA	Prop. Dir.	Designer	Staff
1. Staff meeting	0.25	I											A	P/W	I	C		
2. Develop specification	0.5	I												P	I		W	I
3. Design options	4.0		I————			I											P/W	I
4. Agree options	0.25						I						D	P	I	C	I	I
5. Produce drawings	5.0							I—————————				I		C			P/W	

Time (days) Gantt chart

Responsibility — Team: Est. mgr, Est. officer, Est. PA — Other: Prop. Dir., Designer, Staff

Develop Implementation Plans: Resource Requirement List

What it is

Much of the planning and estimating up until now will have been done without considering resources. This information needs to be incorporated once the responsibility has been completed, so that dependencies and potential obstacles can be identified.

How to use it

1. Take the task plan for each key activity in turn. Add additional columns as shown on the pro forma which follows.

2. Identify the resource required to complete the task – raw materials/systems/specialist help/money/equipment, etc.

3. Clarify exactly when each resource needs to be available.

4. Check on availability.

5. If unavailable, find out why – lead time/other commitments/ out of stock, etc, etc.

6. Determine what you can do to try to resolve the situation.

7. Take appropriate action.

8. Note the response on the chart.

9. If the resource is still unavailable, adjust the task schedule as necessary and inform those who need to know.

10. Look out for resource which may be required for more than one key activity at the same time. If there is insufficient for both, amend the schedules so tasks are completed in series rather than parallel.

RESOURCE REQUIREMENT

Project: (Title)   **Ref No:**

Task	Resource required	Availability	Obstacle/problem?	Action to resolve	Reply

How it helps

A resource requirement list helps to transfer a project plan out of the ideal world into reality. It highlights the potential obstacles and problems which have to be overcome or planned for in developing a schedule.

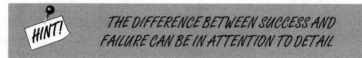

HINT!

THE DIFFERENCE BETWEEN SUCCESS AND FAILURE CAN BE IN ATTENTION TO DETAIL

Develop Implementation Plans:
Cost Breakdown Structure

What it is

Finance is a crucial area for any but the most low level projects. Projects use resources which can be measured in terms of time and materials. They are therefore expected to show an acceptable return and/or be cost efficient in delivering the required results.

How to use it

1. Refer to your task plans and resource requirements charts. Add additional columns as shown below:

Cost breakdown structure						
Project:			Ref No:			
Task	Resource required	Cost	Cost code	Expenditure authorised	Invoice received	Payment

2. For each resource required, calculate the cost (how accurate you need to be will depend on the overall size of the project).

3. Use the pro forma to record the dates when specific costs are authorised, invoices received and payments made.

4. The pro forma can also be used to do a detailed budget and cash flow statement for the project by collating all expenditure against each cost code either in total or month by month.

How it helps

Financial efficiency and effectiveness are almost always important measures of project success. A cost breakdown structure is a useful tool for planning and tracking how you use your money.

Produce a Schedule

What it is

No project should be undertaken without a schedule. A project schedule brings together:

- the key activities and tasks
- how long each activity and task will take
- responsibilities
- resources required.

The main purpose of a schedule is to obtain a clear picture of:

- the order of tasks
- when tasks will be done
- inter-dependencies between activities and tasks
- the total elapsed time, taking into account the availability of appropriate resources.

Once completed the schedule can also be used for ongoing monitoring and control of the project.

There are three ways of producing a schedule. These are:

1. The **GANTT** or bar chart.

2. Critical Path Method (**CPM**).

3. Programme or Performance Evaluation and Review Technique (**PERT**).

For most short projects a simple **GANTT** chart should suffice. However, for larger, more complex and resource consuming projects, the **GANTT** method is likely to be inadequate and the **CPM** or **PERT** more appropriate. This is because a **GANTT** chart is unable to show the inter-dependencies and relationships between activities and tasks. Thus, schedules can be misleading.

CPM scheduling is used where there is familiarity with the tasks involved, because they have been done many times before. Time estimates are thus based on historical data.

PERT employs statistical probability analysis in circumstances in which a project is likely to involve activities or tasks for which no previous record or experience exists. Of the two **PERT** is:

- more time-consuming and complicated because it involves calculating three time estimates to arrive at one for each activity

- open to criticism on the basis that the estimates are all 'guesses' and the use of a composite weighted gross may be no better than taking the most likely estimate in the first place.

PERT is beyond the scope of this Toolbox.

How to use it

1. Review the descriptions of **GANTT** and **CPM**.

2. Decide which one of these is likely to be most appropriate for your needs on the basis of the scale and complexity of your project.

3. Refer to the detailed tool description in this Toolbox.

4. Use the tool to develop your project schedule.

5. If you feel neither is adequate, investigate the use of a **PERT** software package.

How it helps

The schedule is the culmination of all your project planning. It documents what is to be done; when; by whom; with what resource and for how long. It is essential for planning, monitoring and reviewing projects.

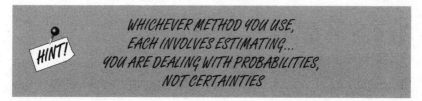

WHICHEVER METHOD YOU USE,
EACH INVOLVES ESTIMATING...
YOU ARE DEALING WITH PROBABILITIES,
NOT CERTAINTIES

Gantt Chart

What it is

A Gantt Chart is a simple charting technique to illustrate actions against time, and dependencies between different actions. It is similar to a Critical Path Analysis.

How to use it

1. Brainstorm tasks to be done.

2. Sequence them – look out for dependencies.

3. Size them – in terms of elapsed time.

4. Display on a Gantt Chart, spread between start and end times.

5. Check feasibility against overall time available.

Example of a Gantt Chart: project to improve telephone response times

Months

Tasks	J	F	M	A	M	J	J	A	S
Review answering process	■								
Document best practice	■								
Train all users in process		■							
Review equipment needs			■						
Identify and agree equipment upgrades				■	■				
Install new equipment						■			
Review switchboard resource reqs						■			
Train all users in equipment							■		
Improve cover arrangements							■		
Train new 'cover' operators							■	■	
Review performance			■			■			■

How it helps

A Gantt Chart identifies all the tasks to be done and when they can start and need to finish to complete a project on time. Once complete, the chart can be used for reviewing progress and amending plans as necessary.

Critical Path Analysis

What it is

Critical Path Analysis is a way of ordering tasks according to dependencies and time taken. It is therefore useful as a planning technique as well as a monitoring technique, particularly on more complex projects. Critical Path charts are also referred to as Arrow Diagrams or Process Decision Programme Charts. They are similar in many ways to Gantt Charts. A Critical Path Analysis shows in a network diagram:

- the critical tasks in terms of impact on total project time

- the most effective way to schedule tasks to achieve the earliest possible target date.

How to use it

1. Brainstorm all the tasks necessary to complete a project (write these on Post-it® Notes, it will save time later).

2. Identify how long each task will take (elapsed time) and record this on the Post-it®.

3. Arrange the Post-its® on a large piece of paper or a board in the order in which tasks can be executed. Start from the left hand side or top. Look for dependencies and also the possibility of parallel tasking. Remove unnecessary tasks and add any which have been missed.

 ALWAYS USE THE SAME UNIT OF TIME FOR EACH TASK

4. Link the Post-it® Notes with lines to show the order in which tasks will be tackled. Use arrows to show the direction of dependencies.

5. Number the Post-its® to show the order in which tasks can be executed.

6. The critical path is the shortest line (in terms of elapsed time) of arrows through the diagram. This shows the minimum time in which the project can be completed.

7. Tasks on the critical path should be started as early as possible, taking into account dependencies and outside constraints.

8. Regularly review progress against the chart and amend as appropriate, particularly if there has been slippage on the critical path.

For example: setting up a training centre (arrow diagram)

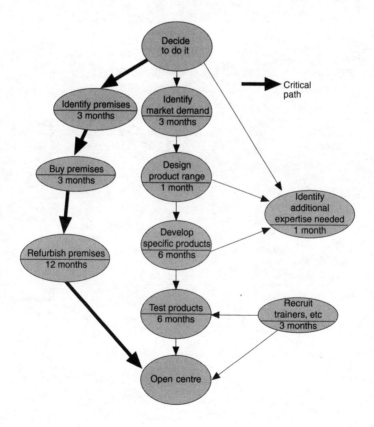

For example: constructing a building (process decision programme chart)

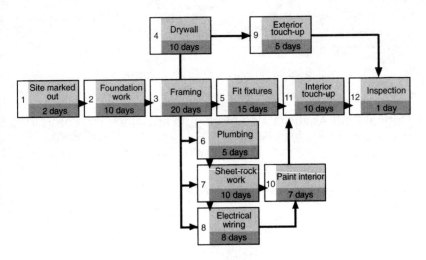

The same data displayed on a Gantt Chart:

Type of work	1	2	3	4	5	6	7	8	9	10	11	12	13
Site marked-out													
Foundation work													
Framework													
Drywalling													
Fit fixtures													
Plumbing													
Sheet-rock work													
Electrical wiring													
Exterior touch-up													
Paint interior wall													
Interior touch-up													
Inspection													

(Tasks / Weeks)

How it helps

Critical Path Analysis is a useful tool for determining the shortest time for achieving a particular task or project and the sequence of events and timing which must take place to achieve this.

If a project falls behind the critical path, the technique can be used to re-estimate the finish time.

A Critical Path Analysis also highlights any slack time around tasks not on the critical path which gives flexibility on when they can be done.

Draft Contingency Plans

What it is

This tool will help you to prevent problems during your project and to anticipate how to react should problems arise.

How to use it

1. Use **SWOT** analysis to assess the robustness of your project plan (see the *Solve that problem!* Toolbox for more details).

STRENGTHS	WEAKNESSES
Project plan strengths	Project plan weaknesses
OPPORTUNITIES	THREATS
'External' opportunities to support or help the project	'External' threats which could jeopardise the project

2. Focus on the threats and weaknesses you have identified and come up with additional actions you can take to overcome and avoid them.

3. For the most serious or complex weaknesses or threats use *Cause and Effect Analysis.*

    Use the tool to identify the causes of the problem(s) and go on to plan what you can do to avoid or manage them. Alternatively use '*Asking Why* ' to dig into specific areas. Keep asking why until you really understand the cause of significant problems.

For example:

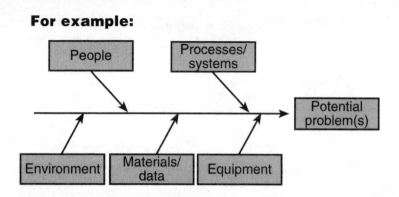

4. Use 'what if?' analysis to identify potential problems.

   Brainstorm possible problem scenarios that might arise over the life of your project. Record all of the ideas on a flip chart; select the most critical items and prepare contingency plans for dealing with the issues – both in terms of prevention and correction.

5. For each key activity ask 'what could go wrong?'. For the most serious situations, again identify steps you can take to avoid them happening or to mitigate their effects if they arise.

6. Use a simple pro forma to capture your work.

7. Keep your chart to hand to help you take corrective action if problems do occur.

8. As your project progresses, repeat the process to ensure your plan is still relevant.

How it helps

Contingency planning is about having plans to deal with problems that you have been unable to prevent. Clearly, you cannot have plans for every possible eventuality. Rather plans should be prepared for the most likely problems that will have significant impact on the project.

CONTINGENCY PLANNING

Project:
Prepared by: Date:

Potential problem	Solution options	Actions taken

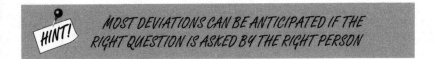

HINT! *MOST DEVIATIONS CAN BE ANTICIPATED IF THE RIGHT QUESTION IS ASKED BY THE RIGHT PERSON*

5 Implement

Support Implementation

What it is

Successful project implementation is often complex and difficult. Project managers must attend to a variety of human, financial and technical factors.

In reality, implementation is inseparable from monitoring and control as the 'doing' and 'checking' happen alongside each other.

Basically implementation is about getting the work done according to plan and ensuring that a number of things are in place to support this activity and manage the consequent changes.

This tool gives a checklist of the things you need to consider to support a successful implementation.

How to use it

1. Review the following checklist.

2. Identify which elements you feel are in place and working successfully.

3. Identify those elements you need to work on to improve the way implementation is going.

4. Refer to other more specific tools as appropriate to work out what to do.

Effective implementation needs:

✔ *An effective communications system*: knowing what should be communicated, to whom, by whom, when, what outcomes are required, etc

✔ *Effective teamwork*: what training, support, review mechanisms are in place. Is the responsibility chart working?

✔ *Information systems*: have measures been agreed? How will data be captured, who will do it? How will it be done? How will it link into the communications system?

✔ *Contingency planning*: has this been done thoroughly enough? How are you dealing with unforeseen problems?

✔ *Progress monitoring and review*: is the planned frequency and format working?

✔ *Customer focus*: is the focus on customer and/or end users views and needs being maintained through regular checking and feedback?

✔ *Working conditions*: are the working conditions for team members adequate?

✔ *Legal and health and safety*: is full compliance to all legal and health and safety requirements being achieved?

How it helps

Successful implementation will be a product of good planning and good monitoring and control. This tool will help you to check that the most important angles have been covered.

6 Monitor and report progress

Review Your Current Approach

What it is

Progress monitoring and reporting is essential to ensure *project control*. Monitoring should tell you:

- is the work being done within the estimates?
- will each activity be completed on schedule?
- is the quality of work within specification?
- are the expected results being achieved?
- are there other changes or special problems?

Knowing these on a regular basis allows you to take timely corrective action which may involve (in order of decreasing acceptability):

- rearranging the workload
- putting in more resource or effort
- moving the target completion date(s)
- lowering your targets.

In its basic form, a project control system can be viewed as a simple process.

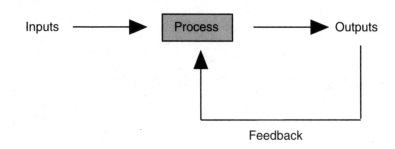

The process should follow a number of principles.

This tool gives you a checklist to compare your current approach with these principles.

How to use it

1. Identify the information you need to track your project in terms of:

- progress towards the objectives (ie improved performance or problem resolution)
- completion of specific tasks/key activities
- efficient use of resources
- adherence to time schedules
- effective team working.

2. Decide how to get this data and use it on a regular basis.

3. Design a process for achieving this using the following checklist:

✔ Control work – not workers

✔ Base control on completed work

✔ Base the control of complex work on motivation and self-control. The people doing the work should control it

✔ Build in the means of gathering control data into the project work process

✔ Ensure control data goes to the person who does the work

✔ Design the control system for the routine, ie not for exceptional issues requiring special handling

✔ Define the criteria for control in the early stages of the project before work starts

✔ Incorporate maintenance of data on performance of the project management process, (including team dynamics) into the control system

---

4. Check that your proposed control system also meets the four basic requirements in that it will allow you to:

- ✔ Plan performance
- ✔ Observe actual performance
- ✔ Compare actuals and plans
- ✔ Adjust as required

5. Finally, ensure that your system is:

- ✔ Focused on priorities
- ✔ Responsive, ie initiates corrective action
- ✔ Timely – no unnecessary delays
- ✔ User friendly
- ✔ Flexible
- ✔ Simple and clear

How it helps

An effective control system is timely, flexible, simple and user friendly. It should also focus on the most important areas of the project. This tool will help you assess how well your approach meets these criteria.

> **HINT!** AN EFFECTIVE CONTROL SYSTEM WILL REDUCE YOUR STRESS LEVEL BECAUSE YOU WILL KNOW WHAT'S HAPPENING

Use Progress Reports

What it is

Progress reports should be made on a copy of the project plan so that whenever one is prepared, it is immediately compared to the plan. This will keep the focus and attention on what matters.

Reports should be prepared at regular intervals. In practice, it should be more often at the detailed action parts of the project to ensure that the data can be used to initiate corrective action in time. As a guide, reports might be produced monthly for the major objectives/key activities progress and weekly for the detailed task level.

Typical contents

The project report is really a mini audit or assessment of where things are at. Some of the key items to cover in preparing a report will include:

- Current project status: How much on track to cost, time and quality is the project?

- Future status: What is the best forecast of what is expected to happen in terms of deviations in the schedule, cost, performance or scope of the project? What specifically will this mean?

- Status of critical tasks: What is happening about particularly critical or sensitive tasks? High risk tasks and those being performed by external agencies or subcontractors over which the project manager has limited control, should also be given special attention.

- Risk assessment: Are any new risks being identified that may impact on any aspects of the project?

- Information relevant to other projects: What has been learned in terms of project strengths and areas for improvement that should be applied to other current or imminent projects in the organisation?

Format

As a rule, the information in a progress report should be organised so that planned versus actual results can be easily compared. Significant deviations should be highlighted and remedial action points clearly identified. Many of the project management software packages that can be purchased contain standardised report formats and pro formas.

Process

Progress reports on activities should be produced by the project member responsible and discussed constructively at project team meetings. Reports on key activities will be prepared by the project team leader and discussed with the team prior to being submitted to/discussed with the project sponsor or commissioner.

Types of report

For *Quality improvement* projects, progress reports are usually linked to the 13 steps of the PDCA cycle and an example of this format is given.

For *conventional projects*, the progress report format will be different but may be incorporated as part of a Quality improvement project reporting process.

Examples of progress report formats for reporting against key activities and task plans/schedules are shown.

IMPROVEMENT PROJECT PROGRESS REPORT

Project Title:		Date:
Leader:	Sponsor:	
Facilitator:	Line manager:	

	Current status:	Identify the progress of your project by ticking the appropriate box corresponding to the current style within the PDCA cycle.
Project status	**Please tick the relevant number on the PDCA cycle**	PLAN DO CHECK ACT 1 2 3 4 5 6 7 8 9 10 11 12 13 ☐ ☐ ☐ ☐ ☐ ☐ ☐ ☐ ☐ ☐ ☐ ☐ ☐
	Do you have a project plan? Yes No ☐ ☐	**If no, why not? – explain** You may not have an implementation because of your current progress through the PDCA cycle (ie stages 1 – 6). Detail here when you expect to have a plan and any constraints that are causing you delay.
	If you have a project plan, are you on time? Yes No ☐ ☐	**If no, why not? – explain** Detail the reason(s) for deviation from the project plan. – Has a restriction caused a delay? – Has it been necessary to change the original plan?
Are we on schedule?	**If you are not on time, what is/are the reason(s): eg Restrictions Money? Help needed? Others?**	**Please explain** Use this space to expand on the reason(s) for delay.
What have we achieved?	**What are your recent achievements?**	**Please explain** Detail the team's achievements since your last report.
What next?	**What is your next step?**	**Please explain** Detail the actions agreed by the team and the expected completion dates.
Comments & review	**General comments on:** **eg** **Benefits quantified** **Measures/monitors** **Barriers/constraints** **Help required** **Project plan and milestones** **Other**	Though not mandatory, this section is important! Use this space to make general comments on the progress of the project. This should assist you in ensuring that the team is working towards its goals and that the terms of the original Improvement teams proposal are being/will be met. **Continue on reverse if necessary**
Press on		

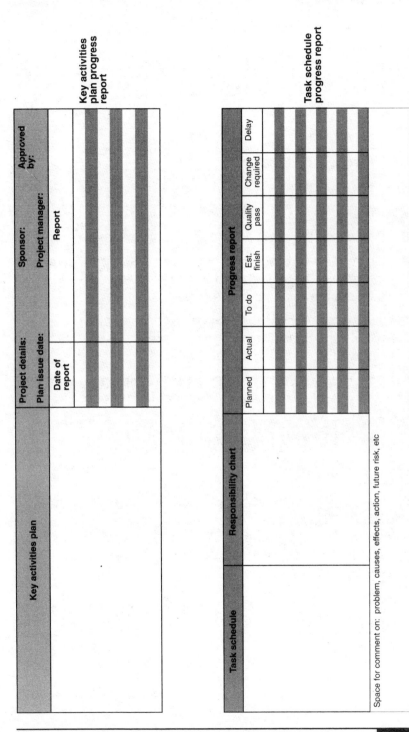

Key activities plan	Project details:	Sponsor:	Approved by:
	Plan issue date:	Project manager:	
	Date of report	Report	**Key activities plan progress report**

Task schedule

| Responsibility chart | | | | | | Progress report | | | | |

| | | Planned | Actual | To do | Est. finish | Quality pass | Change required | Delay | **Task schedule progress report** |

Space for comment on: problem, causes, effects, action, future risk, etc

How to use it

1. Clarify who you need to report to outside of the project team.

2. Identify the type of report you need to produce given the nature of your project.

- Single or multi-level?
- Tabular or text?
- Frequent or occasional?
- Level of detail?
- Author(s)?

3. Decide on the specific information you need to report.

4. Design an appropriate format for the report given the information to be included. Ensure it is as easy and quick as possible to complete and read.

5. Develop a process for gathering, collating and presenting the information. The more this happens automatically as a result of tasks being done, the better.

6. Ensure everyone in the team and the recipients understand the content, process and format of the reports.

7. From time to time review the effectiveness of the reporting process and adjust as necessary.

How it helps

Progress reports keep everyone informed of what is happening and allow ongoing adjustment of plans and resources. Team members find the process of producing reports a helpful discipline to keep things moving and on target.

Maintain a Project Log

What it is

The main purpose of a project log is to monitor the process of the project in a qualitative way so that important management issues can be dealt with and a useful source of information is accumulated for future project process improvement.

The project log records how each step in the project process has been performed with brief notes on strengths and weaknesses, plus action points for addressing the issues. This can then form the basis for improvement.

How to use it

1. Decide whether or not to keep a project log.

2. Design an appropriate format and process bearing in mind:

   - it should have a format and structure along the lines of the example shown on the next page

   - it must be action focused, ie used to resolve the issues

   - it should include hard data as well as opinions.

3. Set aside time in your regular meetings to review and deal with the unresolved issues that are identified in the log.

4. Use specific tools from the *Solve that problem!* Toolbox such as Affinity diagrams or Cause and Effect Analysis to structure your discussions.

5. Agree what specific actions need to be taken to tackle the issues.

How it helps

A project log is a useful tool to help the project team continuously improve the way it is tackling a project.

Project log: Phase 2: Preliminary brief	Project title:		Prepared by: E d Gogh		
		Key points			
Entry date	Item	Pluses	Minuses	Action	Rsp
6/4 (1st monthly meeting)	1) Team membership	Size – six people; good size	Took too long to agree. Two people also on another team – conflict of meeting dates.	Begin discussions earlier on membership. Introduce guidelines on team membership. Set maximum number of teams per person.	JP/Top team RST Top team
	2) Draft brief	Draft available for early discussion	Poor definition of objectives. Unclear structure.	Provide worked examples and guidelines on brief structure and content.	PDPT (EdG)
8/5 (2nd monthly meeting)	1) Project team terms of reference	At last confirmed	Too long to arrive. Initial terms weak on scope, boundaries and authority.		
	2) Sponsor and team leader roles				

Hold Review Meetings

What it is

In order to review progress and to discuss any issues arising from project implementation it is essential to have regular review meetings. These meetings are often at two levels:

- Weekly/monthly for the team.
- Monthly/quarterly for the commissioner(s).

This tool outlines what should be covered at these meetings and who should be involved.

How to use it

1. Decide if and how often to hold review meetings.

2. Agree who is responsible for planning and chairing each meeting (this does not always have to be the team leader).

3. Diary dates and book meeting rooms.

4. Prepare agendas and reports as follows:

   ### Weekly/monthly meetings

   These should involve the team members working on a project and are essentially 'local' meetings. They should concentrate on:

   - reviewing results
   - discussing and solving any problems or issues
   - discussing any deviations from key activity targets and the impact this may have on the targets
   - agreeing and assigning actions to:
     - determine the cause of the deviations
     - correct deviations, or bring performance back on target
   - revising targets (where necessary and appropriate)

- defining additional resource requirements, especially those that will have budget implications

- producing the progress report for upward communication.

Monthly/quarterly meetings

These meetings largely follow the format of the weekly/monthly meetings but differ in several important respects:

- They involve the next level of management, ie the commissioner, sponsor and other key stakeholders.

- They are concerned primarily with the progress of the 'high level' project plan, (ie critical path, key activities).

- Discussion and agreement to the revision of targets needs to take place at this level so that any impact can be considered and taken account of – it is possible that the revision of a target may create a need to 'catchball' the change with the project team.

- They should review the project management process as well as the results – learning points should be recorded and shared.

The project team leader will attend this meeting, not the whole project team.

How it helps

Regular meetings give team members an opportunity to review progress with their leader, to coordinate and plan activities and re-focus on goals. Well-run, they can be very motivating. Similarly, review meetings with the project sponsor and/or commissioner helps the team leader focus on what needs to be done next to achieve the agreed results.

The *Build that team!* Toolbox includes guidelines on how to run effective meetings.

Display Progress

What it is

It is helpful to keep a wider audience informed of the progress of a project so they:

- know what's going on

- are able to make constructive comments and suggestions

- are prepared for the impact of implementation

- see an example of the use of PDCA and appropriate tools.

A storyboard is the most successful method of achieving this.

How to use it

1. Prepare a pro forma of a storyboard as shown on the following page (these can be purchased from Quest). Make it as large and clear as possible.

2. Start by filling in the team mission and members (a photograph can be useful).

3. Once your project plan is complete, add in the planned timings for completing each step.

4. As the project team finish each step of the PLAN-DO-CHECK-ACT cycle, summarise what has been done in the relevant box. Display any tools used as appropriate.

5. Display the storyboard where it can be seen by those most likely to be affected. (If necessary, have more than one on display.)

6. Feel free to add extra sheets around the storyboard if you run out of space.

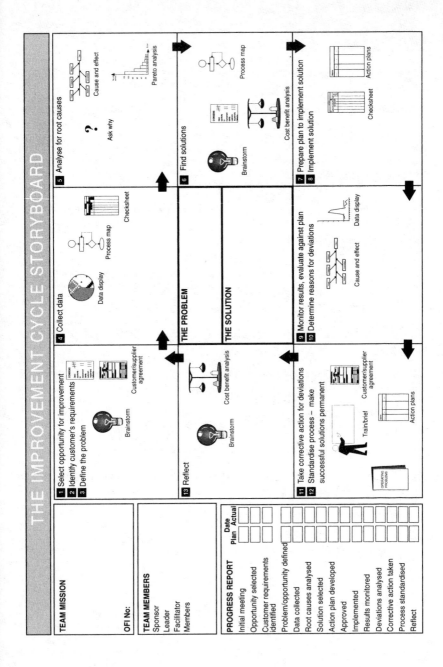

THE IMPROVEMENT CYCLE STORYBOARD

TEAM MISSION

OFI No:

TEAM MEMBERS
Sponsor
Leader
Facilitator
Members

1 Select opportunity for improvement
2 Identify customer's requirements
3 Define the problem

Brainstorm

Customer/supplier agreement

4 Collect data

Data display

Process map

Checksheet

5 Analyse for root causes

Ask why

Cause and effect

Pareto analysis

13 Reflect

Brainstorm

Cost benefit analysis

THE PROBLEM

THE SOLUTION

6 Find solutions

Brainstorm

Cost benefit analysis

Process map

11 Take corrective action for deviations
12 Standardise process – make successful solutions permanent

Train/brief

Customer/supplier agreement

Action plans

9 Monitor results, evaluate against plan
10 Determine reasons for deviations

Cause and effect

Data display

7 Prepare plan to implement solution
8 Implement solution

Checksheet

Action plans

PROGRESS REPORT	Date Plan	Actual
Initial meeting		
Opportunity selected		
Customer requirements identified		
Problem/opportunity defined		
Data collected		
Root causes analysed		
Solution selected		
Action plan developed		
Approved		
Implemented		
Results monitored		
Deviations analysed		
Corrective action taken		
Process standardised		
Reflect		

7. Once the project team has completed its work, leave the white board up for a while until everyone has had the chance to see the finished results. Remember to remove it, however, before it becomes stale and replace it with one for the next project!

How it helps

Storyboards bring projects to life for a wider audience in a way that is structured, easy to follow and quick to read. Use them to communicate with others and to reinforce successful disciplines and tools.

Sort Out Problems

What it is

As problems arise during the course of the project, it will be necessary to apply a discipline and tools for problem-solving. A basic model to follow is given below together with references to appropriate tools contained in the *Solve that problem!* Toolbox.

How to use it

1. Clearly define the problem down to a brief one line statement.

2. Understand the problem and its root cause(s). Use an appropriate tool, such as:

   - Process mapping.
   - Asking why five times.
   - Cause/effect analysis.
   - Affinity diagram.
   - Pareto analysis.
   - Tree diagram.
   - Brainstorming.

3. Brainstorm ideas to tackle the cause(s) of the problem.

4. Select the best idea(s). Use either:

   - Consensus reaching.
   - Decision chart.

5. Develop ideas into specific and actionable solutions.

6. Draw up an action plan.

7. Go do it! (Remember to use the change procedure.)

8. Check results and take corrective action as appropriate.

How it helps

Without action, small problems can grow into major issues and setbacks which can jeopardise your success. This tool helps you to tackle problems methodically and thoroughly so this does not happen.

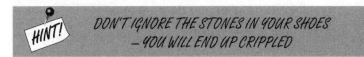

HINT!

DON'T IGNORE THE STONES IN YOUR SHOES
— YOU WILL END UP CRIPPLED

Set Up a Change Procedure

What it is

Changes of some sort will be inevitable over the life of a project. As problems are solved and improvements are made, then the project starts to deviate from the original plans.

Difficulties can arise if there is no specific and agreed change procedure requiring documentation and communication of project changes. The following guidelines may be useful.

How to use it

1. Decide who must approve changes.

2. Agree how changes will be evaluated to assess their impact.

3. Determine how you will keep others informed of agreed changes.

4. Decide if you will inform stakeholders before or after a change is approved.

5. Decide how you will ensure resources are reallocated following a change.

6. Agree how you will document changes to amend project plans.

7. Design a change control format.

Cheapie
brick quote

How it helps

A clear, documented change procedure which is understood and agreed by all stakeholders will help you manage the inevitable changes that are necessary as the project proceeds.

Analyse Deviations

What it is

Deviation analysis combines problem solving and change procedures.

As the implementation stage unfolds, deviations from the plan or expected results will arise.

Deviations above *and* below target should be analysed. The aim is to identify as quickly as possible, the cause of deviation and to take appropriate corrective action. That action then needs to be monitored and if the change is successful, it needs to be established within the process concerned.

This tool outlines a process for achieving this.

How to use it

1. Monitor trends in results and process performance.

- Is the trend in the right direction?
- Are milestones being achieved?
- Is the revised/new process performing within required limits?

   Use *run chart* and *control charts*

2. Identify possible causes of deviation both above and below desired outcomes.

   Use *cause and effect analysis*

3. Collect data on causes.

   Use *check sheets, pareto analysis*

4. Analyse frequency of occurrence and relate to other variables where appropriate.

   Use *histogram* and possibly *scatter diagram*

5. Analyse most frequent causes and take appropriate corrective action.

Use *pareto analysis* and possibly *process mapping* to show change

In summary:

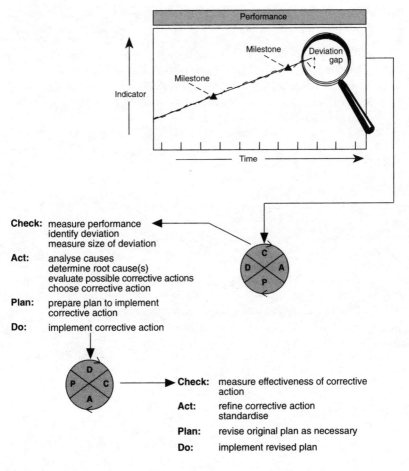

6. Process changes which work then need to be established and standardised through the change procedure. Implications for the forward schedule and resourcing should be estimated and discussed at the review meetings.

How it helps

This tool will help you to take action when actual performance differs from what you planned or expected. The combination of problem solving and the change procedure ensure you maintain control of the project in unexpected circumstances.

APPLY PLAN–DO–CHECK–ACT AT EVERY LEVEL IN THE PROJECT

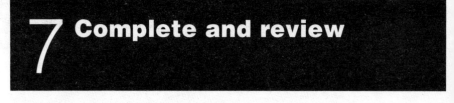

7 Complete and review

Do a Pre-completion Review

What it is

A pre-completion review is primarily for the benefit of the principal customer, the project commissioner. Its purpose is to enable the commissioner to decide:

- if the team has fulfilled its contract, and hence
- whether or not it should be brought to a close.

When a project has been proceeding according to plan, the agenda for the pre-completion review should be straightforward; namely to:

- review with the commissioner(s) the results that have been achieved in relation to the objectives agreed in the contract

- agree on any issues relating to handover and standardisation of changes

- review the effectiveness and efficiency of the main processes in the life of the project

- discuss arrangements for completion and wind-up of the project.

This review should be held as close as possible to the planned termination date for the project, but allowing time for any loose ends to be sorted out before the team disbands.

How to use it

1. Prepare a final report including at least the following:

- **Copy of the original contract and any subsequent amendments**

  This is important because any disputes about the outcome of the project will be more easily resolved if there is a common understanding of the starting point, ie mission, objectives, scope, authorities.

- **Assessment of results in relation to objectives**

  There are three elements:

  - has the required outcome or performance met the primary objective(s)?

  - has this been achieved on budget?

  - has this been achieved on schedule?

- **Deviation analysis**

  Reasons for significant under or over achievement should be identified.

- **Corrective actions**

  Where the team has had to take action to bring a project back on schedule, or performance back into line with what was planned, this should be fully explained as shoulduany cost implications.

- **Current performance or status**

  The content will be dictated largely by the timing of the review, for instance, in relation to handover to others for day to day management of whatever the project team has been responsible for producing.

- **Ongoing progress monitoring**

  Especially in the case of projects whose output is concerned with process improvement, it is extremely important that the project team should have given thought to:

  - how performance of the new/improved process can be monitored on a day to day basis

  - how benefits and savings can be traced and tracked once it has completed its task and been disbanded.

  Amongst other uses, this will help any subsequent assessment of the benefits of an improvement programme.

- **Potential problem or risk assessment**

  Where this is pertinent, then the commissioner should be left in no doubt about what might place the project team's contribution or output at risk.

- **Handover arrangements**

  Where relevant, these should be described. A project commissioner will need to be assured that once the project team has stood down, the new process, facility or whatever, will be properly managed.

Pre-completion review: report format

PROJECT (title) FINAL REPORT	Project contract reference no.
Prepared by: **Date:**	

Introduction:

– copy of Project contract attached

Results assessment versus:

– objectives

– budget

– schedule

– cost savings and benefits analysis
  (can be a separate section)

Significant deviations and corrective actions:

– cause analysis

Current performance status

Monitoring system

Potential risks and sensitivities

Proposed handover arrangements

Completion arrangements

Project assessment (optional)

(a) Overall evaluation:
  – success or failure and why –

(b) Main successes

(c) Disappointments/what could have been done better/obstacles

(d) Lessons for future projects:
  – what could be done differently?

  – recommendations

(e) Team's personal benefits

Project sign-off:

Commissioner(s):	**Team leader:**
Date:	**Date:**
Completion date:	**Post completion review date:**

- **Optional items**

  – *completion*: proposed arrangements for completion, including communication to others

  – *project process assessment*: this is considered more fully under the post-completion review.

2. A pro forma for assembling this information in a simple, clear format is shown on the previous pages.

3. Agree whether or not the report should be presented by the team.

4. Arrange a meeting with your commissioner and sponsor to review the report.

5. Action any outstanding points identified at the meeting.

How it helps

A pre-completion review pulls together loose ends; assesses the success or otherwise of the project and identifies what remains to be done. It is therefore an important step in drawing a project to its close.

 *THERE SHOULD BE NO SURPRISES AT THIS STAGE!*

Use Cost Benefit Analysis

What it is

Cost Benefit Analysis is a technique for comparing the costs of taking a particular course of action with the financial benefits achievable from the outcome. It is a method of assessing the viability of the course of action in monetary terms. It does not include all types of costs and benefits for example – in terms of customer satisfaction, employee morale or environmental sensitivity and is therefore best used in conjunction with other decision making tools.

How to use it

1. Decide on the period over which the Cost Benefit Analysis will be performed.

2. Identify all of the factors involved which will incur costs or provide benefits. Brainstorming can be used at this stage.

3. Separate the factors into those that incur cost and those that produce monetary benefit. Be sure to identify hidden costs such as parallel running, maintenance, additional training and so on.

4. Assess each of the factors and estimate a monetary value.

5. Add the total costs and the total benefits.

For example: purchase of a small computer

Costs (£)	Year					Total
	1	2	3	4	5	
– Purchase of equipment	1000	–	–	–	–	1000
– Less trade in	200	–	–	–	–	200
– Net cost of purchase	800	–	–	–	–	800
– Maintenance contract	–	150	150	150	150	600
– Training	400	100	100	100	100	800
– Software	500	–	–	200	–	700
– Total costs	1700	250	250	450	250	2900

Benefits (£)	Year					Total
	1	2	3	4	5	
Staff savings	2000	2700	2700	2700	2700	12800
Reduced consumables	400	800	800	800	800	3600
Total benefits	2400	3500	3500	3500	3500	16400

Analysis

Benefit to cost ratio $=$ $\dfrac{\text{Value of benefits}}{\text{Total costs}} = \dfrac{16400}{2900} = 5.6:1$

Net annual benefit $=$ Annual benefit – Annual cost
(First year) $=$ $2400 – 1700 = £700$

Net annual benefit $=$ $\dfrac{\text{Total benefits – Total costs}}{5}$
(Average of all years)

$= \dfrac{16400 - 2900}{5} = £2700$

How it helps

This technique can be used to compare alternative solutions in conjunction with evaluating the non-financial benefits, in order to objectively identify the best course of action. Cost Benefit Analysis is also commonly used to evaluate the results of a particular course of action.

Offer a Presentation

What it is

One powerful way to recognise the contribution of team members is to get **the team** to present its results to the commissioner as a group with each member having a part to play – even if it is only putting the visual aids onto the projector. This team effort is surprisingly effective in raising commitment and enthusiasm.

How to use it

1. Choose an anchorperson for the presentation.

2. Share out the work:
   - Preparation of information.
   - Delivery.
   - Preparing visual aids.
   - Writing handouts.
   - Organising refreshments and facilities.

3. Rehearse to check
   - Timings.
   - Individual contributions.
   - Logic and continuity.

4. Decide when to take questions.

5. Do it!
   - Acknowledge contributions to the project.
   - Emphasise achievements and benefits.
   - Include learning points.

To ensure you get your message across:

6. Review how it went as a team.

- ✔ Say what you are going to say
- ✔ Say it
- ✔ Then say what you have said
- ✔ Confirm conclusions and actions
- ✔ Use examples, anecdotes and humour to keep it interesting
- ✔ Always use some form of visual aid
- ✔ Involve your audience wherever possible

How it helps

Presentations are an effective and enjoyable form of communication. They can bring reports to life and allow two-way discussion. At the end of a project, a presentation is a way of recognising the team and energising others to take action.

Complete the Work

What it is

If the project planning and progress monitoring has been thorough and well maintained there should be no difficulty in tidying up the loose ends. Either before or straight after the presentation of the team's report to its commissioner, all outstanding work should have been completed. Some actions may come out of the review presentation, otherwise the team should be in a position to close.

The responsibility for ensuring that this happens is largely that of the team leader, but the commissioner/sponsor can play a key part.

How to use it

1. Identify what needs to be done. Use the example on the next page to stimulate your thoughts.

2. Develop a detailed action plan.

3. Agree who will do what.

4. Set a final review date to sign off the project when all that remains is the celebration!

How it helps

Loose ends have a nasty habit of tripping others up. This tool will help and encourage you to finish everything off and tidy up before moving on.

Outstanding actions (example)	Responsibility
Prepare a completion plan specifically to cover all outstanding work and to identify loose ends	TL
Terminate any temporary customer-supply agreements, eg for provision of data and facilities	TL
Clear any outstanding project cost and budgetary issues	TL/SP
Prepare phase out/run-down schedule	TL
Make arrangements for smooth re-absorption of team members into normal work, especially those who have had significant involvement	PC/SP/TL
Begin to phase team members back into their normal (or new) jobs as soon as is practical	PC/SP/TL
Holding meetings with team members who still have outstanding tasks, using WBS as basis for finalising outstanding work	TL
Prepare handover WBS and schedule as appropriate	TL
Prepare, agree and issue communication about completion	PC/SP/TL
Display and publicise results	TL
Hold a celebration	TL

TL   team leader
SP   sponsor
PC   project commissioner

Handover

What it is

Not all projects will involve a handover, but particularly for large scale capital projects, handover can be an extremely formal and detailed part of the project plan. Sign-off can be a significant event with transfers of major outputs and responsibilities.

For most improvement projects, the emphasis should be on ensuring that any changes to processes are understood, have been documented and standardised.

How to use it

1. Agree a handover/transition plan with the people to whom operational responsibility will be passed.

2. Brief these people and their staff thoroughly on the new process and what needs to be done.

3. Provide adequate training to ensure all concerned can operate the new process/equipment, etc.

4. Rewrite procedures to reflect the new process as necessary. Ensure the new documents have an appropriate version control.

5. Agree a monitoring system and procedures to ensure there is no drift back to old ways and deviations are quickly addressed.

6. Agree a clear cut-off date from when operational responsibility will be assumed.

7. Communicate to other parties as necessary the arrangements for handover and changing responsibilities.

How it helps

A smooth handover will ensure that your work is not lost or wasted and will help others to really benefit from what you have done.

Celebrate!

What it is

After putting a great deal of effort into a project which has achieved the expected results, it is appropriate to celebrate in some way in order to:

- thank the team for their efforts and contributions
- recognise what has been achieved
- encourage team members to join other projects
- encourage others to get involved in improvement activities
- communicate to others what has been achieved.

This tool outlines some ways in which to celebrate and recognise success.

How to use it

1. Review the following ways to celebrate:

✔ Send letters (from the leader, sponsor or commissioner) thanking all involved

✔ Put up a completed storyboard in a permanent position showing what has been done. Include a team photo

✔ Organise an article and/or photo to go in the company magazine

✔ Have a party/drink/meal together

✔ Give the team token presents as a thank you

✔ Organise a visit to another site/conference exhibition, etc that is relevant

✔ Enter the team for an external competition or conference so they can present their work to others

---

✔ Arrange for the team to visit customers or suppliers to present their work or see how it is being applied

✔ Mention the project at other meetings and give credit to those involved

✔ Arrange appropriate training and development to build on new skills/interests

✔ Ask members to be involved in another project

✔ Organise a formal award ceremony. Get someone senior to present certificates or awards. Ensure this is publicised

✔ Promote or nominate for promotion those who have made outstanding contributions

2. Given the size and complexity of your project, decide which of these would be appropriate.

3. Be sure to be fair and consistent with how other projects are handled.

4. It is most important that what is done is valued by the recipients. If necessary ask them what they would like.

5. Do it!

How it helps

Projects can be very demanding of time, energy and commitment. An appropriate celebration recognises this and will help to ensure those involved leave the project feeling positive about it and wanting to contribute further. It also should encourage others to get involved in the future.

Do a Post-completion Review

What it is

In some respects, this is an optional last step in the life of a project. If a project has successfully met its objectives, reported back to its commissioner, ensured standardisation of changes, conducted a smooth handover, secured sign-off, celebrated its success and effectively disbanded itself, what more remains?

The answer is twofold:

- Being certain that the project was conducted as it should have been and that the results are sustainable.

- Capitalising on learning.

How to use it

1. Decide whether to approach this as a formal audit or a 'friendly' inquest.

Audit

- Gives an objective view of how well a project was managed; its benefits and impact.

- Conducted by an independent party.

- Can be time consuming and costly.

- Can engender defensive reactions.

- Usually only used for large, complex and costly projects.

Friendly 'inquest'

- Done by the project team (although customers and suppliers can be involved).

- Involves pooling experience to improve the project management and improvement processes.

- Quite cheap but subjective.

2. Agree the inputs, such as:

- Project log.
- Questionnaire/interviews for team members.
- Questionnaire/interviews with selected customers, suppliers.
- Control data.

3. Review the material and draw conclusions, in areas such as:

- Effectiveness and efficiency.
- Robustness and value of the contract.
- Quality of support received.
- Problems of personal time management.
- Resourcing issues.
- Lessons learnt.
- Things which could have been done better.

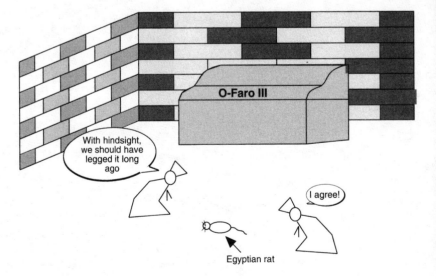

4. Prepare a report proposing improvements to project management processes and giving advice and guidance to future project teams. Alternatively this information can be included in the pre-completion review if the timing is right.

How it helps

A post-completion review draws out the learning from the project and helps to ensure that this is used and passed on to help others avoid the same pitfalls and to benefit from your experience.

8 Manage multi-projects

Define Your Problem

What it is

Multi-project environments as such are not problematic providing due thought has been given to their organisation and control. Indeed, in some circumstances, there is a strong case to be made for driving growth and improvement by projects. However, when a multiplicity of projects is unplanned and the implications not thought through, the consequences can be severe, including:

- individual overload and stress
- falling (service) standards
- meetings proliferation
- frustrated employees/customers/suppliers
- unnecessarily long projects
- top management attention diverted
- rising costs, overrun budgets
- fuzzy priorities
- project team recommendations are approved, but somehow don't get implemented
- some departments overloaded.

There are four areas to focus on to counteract these potential problems:

- People loading.
- Functional loading.
- Project tracking.

- Strategy for organising projects.

Each concerns the capacity of the organisation to deliver high quality results through projects.

How to use it

1. Decide whether your concern is:

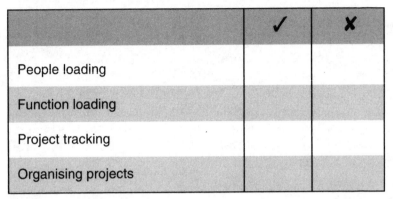

	✓	✗
People loading		
Function loading		
Project tracking		
Organising projects		

2. Refer to the specific tool(s) in this section which are most relevant.

3. Go do it!

4. Review whether or not your problem has eased or whether you need to tackle other aspects of your approach to project management.

How it helps

However well run an individual project, you will have problems if there are too many of them or the same people or departments are stretched more and more thinly to resource them. The tools in this section will help you to manage the multi-project environment.

Control People Loading

What it is

This is a vital consideration whichever type of organisation is put in place, but no more so than when much, if not all, project activity is resourced from within existing capacity. Thus, in addition to their current jobs, people are expected to participate in one or more project teams.

The *project involvement table* can be used before a period of multiple project activity to plan loading and as a check during that period.

How to use it

1. Identify the individuals you are concerned about.

2. Identify the projects they are involved in over a given period.

3. Build up a matrix to show their involvement:

For example: Project involvement table

Person \ Project	Period: Jan - March					
	Lead time 1.1	Stock accuracy 4.4	Raw material suppliers 1.5	Manf.cycle times 4.1	Warehouse customisation 3.1	Planning process 2.2
J Potter	▲	■	○	▲	○	■
S C Stiff	▲	▲	○	○	○	▲
C C Lass	■	■	▲	■	○	▲
J C Brown	○	○	○	○	▲	○
A K Smith	■	▲	▲	▲	○	■
I T Fright	■	▲	○	○	▲	■

Involvement symbols

▲ significant   ■ some   ○ little or none

4. This simple approach shows individual loadings at a glance. If this is insufficient, however, a more sophisticated approach is provided in the *people loading table*. This links the degree of involvement by project more precisely to the weeks in question.

For example: Project loading table

People	Weeks								
	1	2	3	4	5	6	7	8	9
J Potter	▲ 1.1 ■ 2.2	▲ 1.1 ■ 2.2	▲ 1.1 ■ 2.2 ■ 4.4	▲ 1.1 ■ 2.2 ■ 4.4 ▲ 4.1	▲ 1.1 ■ 4.4 ▲ 4.1	▲ 1.1 ■ 4.4 ▲ 4.1	H O L I D A Y	▲ 1.1 ▲ 4.1	▲ 1.1 ▲ 4.1
S C Stiff	▲ 1.1	▲ 1.1	▲ 1.1 ▲ 4.4 ■ 2.2	▲ 1.1 ▲ 4.4 ■ 2.2	▲ 1.1 ▲ 4.4 ▲ 2.2	▲ 1.1 ▲ 4.4 ▲ 2.2	▲ ▲ 4.4 ▲ 2.2	▲ 1.1 ▲ 4.4 ▲ 2.2	■ 1.1 ▲ 4.4 ▲ 2.2

Involvement symbols

▲ Significant involvement in project (ref no:)   ■ Some involvement in project (ref no:)

5. Decide what are acceptable limits on involvement. For most purposes, the following approximations of impact upon time can be used:

- 'Significant' = >10% of the person's time per project.
- 'Some' = 5-10% of the person's time per project.

6. Using these definitions a project loading matrix can be developed as a basis for prescribing the limits of people involvement.

For example: Project loading matrix

Number of projects	▲ – significant involvement				
	4	3	2	1	0
4	●	●	●	●	☹
3	●	●	●	☹	☹
2	●	●	●	☹	●
1	●	●	☹	●	●
0	●	☹	☹	●	/////

(row label on left axis: ■ – some involvment)

Involvement

▲ 'significant' >10 of normal time   ■ 'some' 5-10% of normal time

Warning

● 'red' – loading too high

☹ 'amber' – loading becoming problematic

● 'green' – loading OK

7. Use the matrix to manage personal involvement in projects, remembering that individuals react differently to pressure and have different work rates.

8. Once all individuals are fully occupied, you have then simply to decide:

- Can you 'buy-in' temporary help?
- If not, which projects will have to be delayed?

How it helps

This tool will help you to manage individual involvement in projects rather than just allowing pressure and stress to build up by ignoring the situation. It will force you to consider the full range of potential project members rather than just those few who keep being asked to get involved.

 DON'T JUST GO FOR THE OBVIOUS 'STARS', THERE WILL ALSO BE LOTS OF HIDDEN TALENTS

Monitor Functional Loading

What it is

In a multi-project environment, the problem of project overloading can occur at the functional/departmental as well as the individual level. Just as individuals can become overloaded, so too can functions. Particular examples are engineering departments, I.T., finance and, occasionally, legal functions.

The reasons for this are not hard to find. They contain people with technical/professional expertise that can lend itself readily to project-type work. Cross-functional project teams, in particular, tend to draw heavily for their members from the same areas, thus increasing the likelihood of stretching a department's resources beyond sensible limits.

The consequences of functional overload are not dissimilar to those of personal overload:

- Service to internal and external customers suffers.

- Response to project team requirements lengthens.

- Priorities become confused.

- Errors can rise.

- Temporary labour and overtime costs can rise.

How to use it

1. Identify all of the projects involving a specific function.

2. Identify who is involved in each; when and for how much time (your estimating will improve with practise).

3. Build up a matrix.

4. Calculate the total resource available for projects in the function each week (take holidays and other commitments into account).

Function/department	LEGAL							
	Estimated resource required (hours)							
Projects	Week							
	1	2	3	4	5	6	7	26
Developing new life product	20	20	20	30	30	30	20	
Purchasing new warehouse	10	10	5	0	0	0	0	
Revising job contracts	5	10	15	15	20	15	10	
Setting up internal enquiry service	15	15	20	20	25	25	25	
Selling old HQ premises	10	10	0	0	5	5	0	
Acquiring new printing operation	25	20	15	10	5	0	0	
Recruiting new lawyer	5	0	0	20	0	0	10	
Total needed	90	85	75	95	85	75	65	
Total available	95	95	95	95	60	60	95	
Surplus/shortfall +/-	+5	+10	+20	0	-25	-15	-30	

5. Highlight weeks where the demand for resource meets or exceeds capacity.

6. For these weeks, consult as appropriate to identify:

- is other 'temporary' resource available?
- can commitments be moved?
- can projects be delayed?

7. Develop a 'warning' system to give early signals of overloading as resource commitments are made.

8. Regularly review forward load and take action as necessary.

How it helps

Individual project commitments can seem small, yet taken together they can lead to promising resource that is not available. This tool will help to prevent this occurring by monitoring functional loading.

FUNCTIONAL OVERLOAD ALL TO EASILY TRANSLATES INTO PERSONAL OVERLOAD

Track Projects

What it is

Keeping track of progress on individual projects will not of itself control their number, but is an essential element in managing the multi-project environment. The needs can vary from one set of circumstances to another.

For example:

- Monitoring improvement projects through a change programme to check progress and involvement.

- Tracking capital expenditure projects for cash flow.

- Tracking merger and acquisition activities to meet key deadlines.

The tracking process and documents used will clearly vary depending on the need.

How to use it

1. Decide what you need to know and why.

2. Decide how to collect and collate the data.

3. Agree who will monitor the system and take action if needed, eg when

   - deadlines are missed

   - budgets are exceeded

   - resources are overstretched

   - projects succeed and need recognition.

4. Design a database that ideally can be interrogated:

   - by topic

   - by person

   - by stage.

5. Design appropriate pro formas and a detailed procedure, for example:

Ref no.	Project title	Sponsor	Team leader	Facilitator	Start date	Planned completion date	On schedule*	Forecast completion date	Final presentation	Issues+

* On schedule? 😀 'ahead' 😐 'on' 🙁 'behind'

+ Must include reasons for behind schedule

How it helps

A tracking system tell you how many projects are underway, who is involved and what stage they are at. Only track, however, if you will take action when needed.

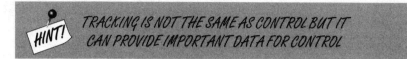

HINT! *TRACKING IS NOT THE SAME AS CONTROL BUT IT CAN PROVIDE IMPORTANT DATA FOR CONTROL*

Organise for Projects

What it is

This tool considers three approaches to organisation structure which each have benefits for project work.

Functional emphasis

Projects are contained within functions and controlled within the line reporting structure. A special 'project' section is sometimes established, for example:

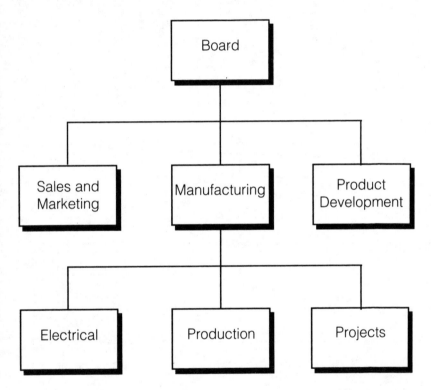

This approach is neat, easy to manage and focused. However, it can be inflexible cross-functional projects are more difficult.

Project emphasis

Projects are usually focused on processes so there is a close fit between them and the work breakdown structure.

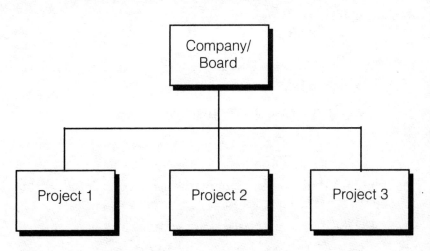

This gives clear roles and focus and resource is available, but again, it can be inflexible.

Matrix

This combines the two other approaches, so people have both functional and task responsibility.

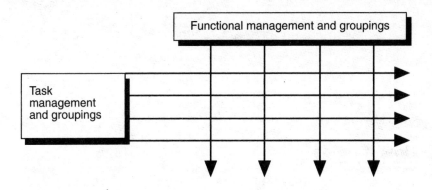

Individuals are seconded to projects as necessary, although there may be some full-time project managers. This approach allows flexible use of resource but priorities and reporting can be confusing.

How to use it

1. Review how you use projects in your organisation. Are they:

- functional/multi-functional?
- major/minor resource commitment?
- linked to processes?
- centrally coordinated?

2. Identify what currently works well for you. What are the strengths of your approach?

3. What are the problems or disadvantages in your approach?

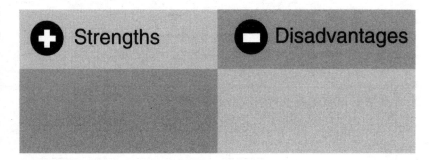

4. Review the alternative approaches. How well would they meet your needs?

5. What would be the optimum solution for your circumstances? (There is no one right answer.)

6. How can you move towards that solution?

How it helps

This tool does not give answers. It can only help you to assess your current approach to linking organisation structure to projects, and how this might be improved.

Rank Projects

What it is

This tool will help you determine the order in which projects should be done by ranking them according to benefits, ease and contribution.

How to use it

1. Complete the list of projects so that all existing projects are included.

2. Rank the list of projects by scoring each project out of ten for:

   • benefit to the bottom line

   • how easy it is to do

   • contribution to the overall improvement goal or any other criteria you may think of.

3. Multiply the three scores to give a score for each project. This can be done on one sheet for each priority area. The maximum score is 1000.

Project	Benefit a	Easy to do b	Contribution to priority area c	Total axbxc
A				
B				
C				
D				

4. Review the resource required for each of the top ranking projects in order to decide whether they can be done in parallel or series.

How it helps

Project ranking by this method is a quick and easy way to aid decision making on a range of project priorities, and it results in some more 'objective' data that can be used to support decisions reached.

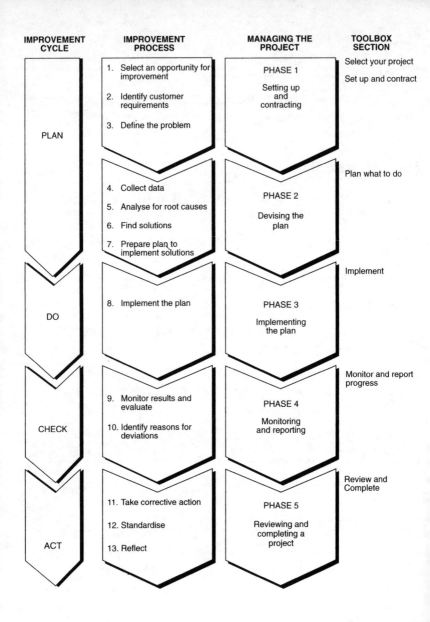

IMPROVEMENT CYCLE	IMPROVEMENT PROCESS	MANAGING THE PROJECT	TOOLBOX SECTION
PLAN	1. Select an opportunity for improvement 2. Identify customer requirements 3. Define the problem	PHASE 1 Setting up and contracting	Select your project Set up and contract
PLAN	4. Collect data 5. Analyse for root causes 6. Find solutions 7. Prepare plan to implement solutions	PHASE 2 Devising the plan	Plan what to do
DO	8. Implement the plan	PHASE 3 Implementing the plan	Implement
CHECK	9. Monitor results and evaluate 10. Identify reasons for deviations	PHASE 4 Monitoring and reporting	Monitor and report progress
ACT	11. Take corrective action 12. Standardise 13. Reflect	PHASE 5 Reviewing and completing a project	Review and Complete